Youth Literature for Peace Education

Youth Literature for Peace Education

Candice C. Carter and Linda Pickett

Contributions by
Shelly Clay-Robison

YOUTH LITERATURE FOR PEACE EDUCATION
Copyright © Candice C. Carter and Linda Pickett, 2014.
Softcover reprint of the hardcover 1st edition 2014 978-1-137-36226-1
All rights reserved.

First published in 2014 by
PALGRAVE MACMILLAN®
in the United States—a division of St. Martin's Press LLC,
175 Fifth Avenue, New York, NY 10010.

Where this book is distributed in the UK, Europe and the rest of the world, this is by Palgrave Macmillan, a division of Macmillan Publishers Limited, registered in England, company number 785998, of Houndmills, Basingstoke, Hampshire RG21 6XS.

Palgrave Macmillan is the global academic imprint of the above companies and has companies and representatives throughout the world.

Palgrave® and Macmillan® are registered trademarks in the United States, the United Kingdom, Europe and other countries.

ISBN 978-1-349-47264-2   ISBN 978-1-137-35937-7 (eBook)
DOI 10.1057/9781137359377

Library of Congress Cataloging-in-Publication Data

Carter, Candice C., 1953–
   Youth literature for peace education / Candice C. Carter and Linda Pickett ; with contributions by Shelly Clay-Robison.
     pages cm
   Summary: "Carter and Pickett explore how educators and families can teach peace education through youth literature and literacy development. Showing how to assess, choose, and make use of literature that can be used to teach both literacy and peace education, they walk through individual methods: recognizing and teaching different portrayals of conflict in youth literature, analyzing characterization, and examining the role of illustrations. Educators who want to incorporate peace education within a broader, literacy-focused curriculum, and peace educators looking for age-appropriate materials and methodologies will find Youth Literature for Peace Education a rich and interdisciplinary resource"—Provided by publisher.
   Includes bibliographical references and index.

     1. Young adult literature—Study and teaching. 2. Peace—Study and teaching. 3. Children's literature—Study and teaching. I. Pickett, Linda. II. Title.

PN1008.8.C37 2014
809'.89282071—dc23   2014015426

A catalogue record of the book is available from the British Library.

Design by Newgen Knowledge Works (P) Ltd., Chennai, India.

First edition: October 2014

10 9 8 7 6 5 4 3 2 1

Contents

List of Tables	vii
Acknowledgments	ix
Introduction	xi
1 Teaching for Peace with Youth Literature	1
2 Characterization	25
3 Diversity	43
4 Language Usage	61
5 Illustrations	81
6 Conflict	105
7 Inclusive Peace Her/History	123
8 Developmental Learning	149
Featured Literature	167
References	181
Name Index	201
Subject Index	209

Tables

1.1 Contexts for peace visions 15
1.2 Pedagogy of peace education 18
5.1 Skill evaluation 92

Acknowledgments

We appreciate many people who supported the production of this book. We are grateful for everyone who supports youth learning about peace and provides literature for that goal.

Introduction

Why combine peace education with literacy? They are interdependent. Peace, wherein life-sustaining needs and human rights are met, enables the development of literacy. The rights of children include education. Yet, many children, in the United States as well as other world regions, are not experiencing those rights. Either they are not in school, or educational programs are not fully developing their literacy skills. In a nation where freedom of speech was legalized, it is important to teach those who do have full opportunities for their education how to read not only the written word but also read about their world. Social literacy involves reading about conflicts and how people responded to them. Human development and maintenance of peace is dependent on the ability to analyze conflict and create responses to it without causing harm.

Literature has a clear role in human development while the record of human accomplishments demonstrates that communication is crucial for peace. The promotion of peace for the well-being of life and its environment occurs in the formal as well as informal education of youth. In the past century, the goal of education for peace expanded beyond faith communities and war zones to government-supported programs along with independent schools. Parents, educators, librarians, and mental health professionals have relied on literature for youth to present the components of peace. This book supports their objectives for using literature. Our intention is reinforcement for their indirect or direct instruction with the use of literature for reading and social literacy.

There are three goals for this book. The first goal is support of education through informed curriculum development and the selection of literature. Information in this book equips consumers of youth literature with considerations for their selection of publications they may optimally use, especially as formal or informal learning material. Just as importantly, developers of youth literature can apply the information contained here for design of content that reinforces peace education. The second goal of enhancing youth literature for peace education includes the educational effects of enjoying good literature in any situation where learning can occur.

There are several teaching opportunities for families, teachers, and others who interact with youth. Education occurs in many ways, including processes that can advance communication skills and social literacy. While youth enjoy observing, hearing read, and reading literature, they can learn about several topics that pertain to peace. The means by which humans deal with conflict are germane to literature and social studies, as well as other disciplines that present problem solving.

Optimally, students have opportunities across subject areas for analysis of how people have responded to problems. Integrated instruction in conflict management is relevant and shows that all factors need attention when solving a problem. Peace education's orientation towards holistic learning with relevant curriculum that includes the current challenges learners have in their society involves more than integrated instruction. A vision of a life without violence includes the fulfillment of evident needs.

The third goal for this book addresses the need for guidelines in peace-oriented education. The dearth of government-prescribed standards with components of peace education undermines publically funded education that connects school support to assessment of those learning outcomes. The contents we provide here fill the gap that is evident in government oversight of peace education. An overview of the book's contents illustrates our objectives in the development of this aid.

Chapter 1 provides rationales and considerations for use of youth literature in peace education. It clarifies learning goals and classifications of conflicts that are evident across the societal spectrum, including particular as well as universal situations where humans have experienced problems. Chapter 2 includes the presentation of diversity in youth literature, including analysis of how it illustrates human differences. Chapter 3 brings attention to characterization in literature and how it relates to structures in a society. Chapter 4 addresses the use of language, which imparts skills as well as information for youth. Chapter 5 gives evaluation questions to ask about the illustrations in the literature and describes the indispensible role of arts in peace development. Chapter 6 supports analysis of how the literature presents conflict and responses to it that advance or undermine the transformation of human interactions. Following up in that vein, Chapter 7 addresses the need for inclusive instruction about humanity's peace-oriented accomplishments. Chapter 8 continues with the theme of development by presenting considerations in the use of literature for teaching all children.

The enhancement of literacies and the creation of literature that enables such learning advance peace. Education for peace is an opportunity that all youth deserve. The information here reinforces everyone in the provision of that prospect.

1
Teaching for Peace with Youth Literature

Quests for peace through education are worldwide. Teaching for peace remains as old as the words and illustrations that express that goal. Awareness of recent methods for that pursuit is the foundation for advancement of peace through education. Literature and art have been the mortar for construction of knowledge, dispositions, and skills needed in peace development. Visual and verbal communication facilitates the awareness needed for understanding. Literature enables that kind of communication for youth. Included in this chapter are rationales for the use of youth literature in peace education and the cultivation of social literacy. A description of peace education precedes the discussion regarding the use of literature as a method to teach peace.

Construal of Peace

Foremost in education is the articulation of clear learning goals and objectives. The construal of peace makes the learning objectives toward that universal goal possible. A plethora of translations for the concept of peace demonstrates its centrality as a human goal and supports articulation of objectives. People worldwide have included the notion of peace in their spiritual as well as faith-based traditions and have recommended means for accomplishing it.

Beyond faith-based instruction, other pedagogies exist that clearly include lessons on peace. The call for such instruction in secular schools has been responsive to the situations in which people live. First, the division of faith-based instruction from public schooling in the United States, for adherence to the national constitution requiring separation of church and state, resulted in the promotion of peace-oriented instruction in government-funded schools. Moral education, which the French sociologist Emile Durkheim (1973) described, has been an initiative to fill the gap that teachings of the church provided the youth in faith-based schools. Teaching the youth appropriate ways to live in their society has included various forms of character education, involving a clarification of values and a promotion of national goals like patriotism.

The construal of peace is contextually responsive as well as value based. The conception envisions the harmonious enactment of multiple values that are evident in conflict. Patriotism, for example, demonstrates the value of preserving a nation, while pacifism exemplifies the value of violence-free resolutions for international conflicts. These values, when combined, result in people becoming conscientious objectors to their involvement in war and serving their government as noncombatants during international crises. The record of how male and female politicians, as well as citizens of a nation, object to war and call for other means of resolving international conflict demonstrates patriotism without violence. The notion of global patriotism evidences another construal of peace, whereby people think beyond nationalism to an inclusive identity that encompasses global and regional unity. Learning about the unfolding of people's identities and how those revelations have affected peace developments includes fascinating stories from world regions. Chapter 7 has more discussion of this record. The present discussion is a brief summary of construing peace in education, especially in secular schools.

Harmonious Living

The vision of people living together in ways that accommodate individual and group differences illustrates the harmony of humanity. The enactment of pluralism supports this harmony through acceptance, regardless of ethnic and cultural identity or physical characteristics. Additionally, the advancing concept in the West, which Buddhists in the East and indigenous populations articulated long ago, that harmony includes all life on this planet, has been more recently, described as sustainability. Harmony of all life forms envisions humans adapting to the ongoing changes of the natural environment and the protection of other species, which humans endanger. Interspecies peace is a form of mutualism involving cohabitation of humans with animals and plants (Andrzejewski, Pedersen, & Wicklund, 2009). Further elaboration of harmony includes life beyond earth. Planning for how to preserve the environments in outer space is another peace initiative (Global Network, 2014). In the pursuit of social, political, environmental, and galactic harmony, inevitable conflicts do not need to result in the destruction of life and the natural conditions that support it. Avoidance of unnecessary conflict is another concept of peace.

Conflict Prevention

Conflicts typically result from unmet needs. Those needs exist in the mind and the physical conditions that influence how people think. The pursuit of peace involves recognition of these needs and proactive responses to them, which result when people are unable to create or carry out ways for fulfilling unmet needs. Psychologists have studied the way minds experience needs and responds to them, as well as how people have thought of conflict responses. The *Journal of Peace Psychology* and other publications offer a window to indirectly observe peace-related behaviors in the face of conflict. Prevention of conflict includes need fulfillment through people sharing ideas about problem prevention and solution.

Their proactive responses, which do not involve any type of violence, build peace.

Avoidance and Repair of Harm

Finding a solution to a problem without harming anyone is another concept of peace. Harm can be psychological or physical. Conflict often evidences harm that has occurred. Work for peace entails recognition of harm indicators. Such endeavors involve thorough analysis of how people might respond to conflict. To avoid harm, there is a need for awareness of the conditions in which people live and of their cultural norms; this awareness is important in responding to the psychological and the material circumstances of conflict.

Fulfillment of Needs

Unmet needs resulting in human violence typically are rooted in conditions that do not sustain survival. Peace is not present when concerns regarding the inability to survive exist. Whether the threats to life are physical or mental, the perception of them reveals conflicts that must be resolved. While physical threats to survival necessitate quick elimination, lack of peace in the psychological realm indicates a peace-building opportunity in that community. When one person has a need that is not met, it can result in that person inflicting self-harm as well as harm to others. Such needs can range from a desire for things, especially in a society characterized by materialism, to dissatisfaction with human interactions. Mental peace results from fulfilling the need for recognition, respect, and the power for self-actualization, among other sources of psychological well-being.

Social and Legal Justice

Social and legal justice indicate needs for peace. Social justice describes the societal conditions that determine personal and group well-being. A state in which there is an obstruction to the means for obtaining well-being, and the right to change the conditions that prevent it, demonstrates injustice. Entrenched in these operations are systemic and structural conflicts. When there is a lack of legal representation and protection, as discrimination within a judicial system evidences, there cannot be social peace. All members of a society need the opportunity for well-being and the power to bring it about.

The fulfillment of everyone's needs occurs through representation. Lacking a voice to express unmet needs impedes peace. Representation of all populations, including those in the environment who cannot speak for themselves in the legal system, such as plants and animals as well as people who do not have fluency in the official language(s) of the government, is essential for peace. Initiatives to represent nature and people in the courts have illustrated this construal of peace. In order to present a conflict and participate in the discussions about how to resolve it, people need power. Lacking that power, the solutions have often failed to sufficiently solve the existing problems and prevent future ones.

Ideas about what constitutes peace are beyond the scope of this publication, which addresses learning. The notion of peace education resulted from the awareness that students who are informed about the many ways in which peace has been created and construed are better prepared for life's challenges. A vision of harmonious living features youth, as well as adults, who are well-versed in peace for preservation and development of it across many aspects of life. The following about education for peace describes some of the learning opportunities youth have been given to fulfill this vision.

Peace Education

People have used the concept of peace to characterize aspects in the personal, cultural, societal, regional, global, and spiritual realms of their lives. People learned lessons on peace through the informal education of social interactions and physical arrangements comprised in their lives, as well as through formal instruction. Informal education happens through observation and interaction. Many people who engage in peace development had role models or mentors who indirectly taught them through their ideas and corresponding actions. The combination of an ideological foundation, a role model or mentor, and motivation for action in the recognition of unmet needs are common backgrounds of peacemakers (Carter, 2014). A close look at the thoughts and actions of high-profile peacemakers typically reveals a desire for improvement and a better life for those in need along with others in the world. While being aware of those important factors in the pursuit of peace, informal and formal instruction occurs through deliberate cultivation of the knowledge and skills that support success. Through sharing information in literature about peace development, the youth can glean the nature of accomplishments toward peace. With guidance, they can formally identify and demonstrate the knowledge, skills, and dispositions that have been useful in the achievement of peace.

Peace education is culturally defined and contextually distinct. In other words, people within a culture identify peace in the enactment of their values and the lifestyles that embody those principles. A contextual factor that determines the lessons is the nature of the conflicts that have been evident in the society. Evidence of bias is one contextual factor. Stereotyping people as problem causers result in facilitating students' critical awareness coupled with motivation and skills to counteract bias in their community (Teaching Tolerance, 2014). This is especially acute in areas where direct violence has left visible harms that make it harder to overcome perceptions of "the other" as troublemakers. Other contextual factors have been the nature of the school that sets out to teach youth about violence prevention and conflict resolution. The approaches have been widely varied, depending on the mission of the school, the pedagogy it typically provides, and the commitment of the school members to educating for peace. When the school mission includes language about conflict and peace, there is a clear rationale for instruction by the school staff and teachers in the many situations in which youth will experience conflict and the need for its peaceful resolution. Notwithstanding the importance of a school mission that articulates the goal of peace, educators who are committed to teaching for peace have found means for accomplishing their goal within institutions where there was no clear rationale for such instruction. One reason for this may be the common goal that educators have for teaching youth about conflict management. While peace education has been comprehensive in schools with supporting missions, it has been viable in all the situations in which youth learn about how humans have solved their problems. By their very nature as institutions that manage the daily lives of their students, schools present many conflict lessons.

Teaching Peace

Educating About Conflict

Teaching youth about conflict occurs informally while they experience and observe the ways people avoid and respond to problems (Carter, 2002; Swick & Freeman, 2004). This includes the use of literature that renders problem-solving strategies. Sources of violence, prevention and ending of violence, management of conflict without harm, and peace her/history are components of social education. Whether or not the use of literature is purposefully instructional, readers and listeners find out about the nature of conflict and ways of responding to it. Hence, the presentation of how people face conflict provides opportunities for demonstrating the development of peace. Literary characters are role models for youth, albeit positive or negative. Explicit instruction with literature enables cultivation of analytical skills when examining how people and characters deal with the conflicts they face. To aid the analysis, peace education provides students with categories for conflict and their management. Those categorizations facilitate the identification of strategies that have been useful in avoiding harmful reactions to conflict, including an existing state of violence in the world and effects on relationships and self. To provide relevance, which is crucial in social education, the formal and informal lessons address situations and populations that relate in the context of the students' lives. Purposefully included are representations of their identities, history, and current, as well as past, situations that members of their culture, community, and nation have faced. Such instruction has variably included revisionist history that presents the involvement and perspectives of dominated peoples, herstory that renders the role of females, as well as males and youth, in the many ways they have been proactive responders to social problems. Recent initiatives to provide conflict instruction are bully education, violence prevention, conflict resolution, along with social and emotional learning (Collaborative for Academic, Social and Emotional Learning, 2014; Johnson & Johnson, 1995; Prothrow-Stith & Spivak, 2005). Most of these approaches to teaching the management of conflict and avoidance of violence demonstrate a vision of human harmony, especially in schools and communities that have a mixture of ethnicities and cultures. The difference of cultural norms in close encounters presents youth with learning opportunities for coexistence.

Coexistence

Youth, and many adults too, need to reach across the cultural borders that they perceive. These borders exist in the alignment of group members and the norms of the group that are different from those of the observer. When the youth have been socialized to think of "the other" as a source of conflict for their identity group, there is a great need for coexistence education. Goals include recognition of and proactive responses to intolerance and injustice, as well as the evidence of ethnocentrism. The development of an ethnorelativistic perception, in which cultural differences are not viewed with a lesser value than one's own norms, occurs through positive descriptions of and exposure to those differences. Youth move from acceptance to accommodation of those differences, and sometimes adaptation to the different norms of others around them. Strategies that have been provided, some free of cost through nonprofit organizations, include contact and conversations with youth who are on the other side of cultural and political borders (Teaching Tolerance, 2014). For consistency of adult modeling, coexistence education happens through a campus. A World of Difference, for example, is a program that includes diversity lessons and analysis of conflicts resolved through proactive responses by all members of the school (Anti-Defamation League, 2014). Comprehensive peace education promotes more than a culture of peace in schools by broadening the lens to view global sites of intolerance and injustice (Reardon, 1988). For example, it promotes instruction about human rights, especially those identified by the United Nations in the Convention on the Rights of the Child (United Nations, 2009). In addition to promoting coexistence with diverse others and the protection of everyone's rights, peace education has been increasing the examination of life circumstances for other species.

Sustainable Living

Ecological security and interdependence have become strands of peace education. Sustainability involves preserving and repairing the natural environment, including the earth and other spaces that humans have affected, together with the regions of their solar system. In the study of the natural world, youth learn about the conflicts in nature such as volcanoes, earthquakes, and the predator-prey relationship, which are part of earth's evolution. In peace education, they are taught about distinctions between human violence to nature and natural evolutionary processes in the physical world. Additionally, they learn the similarities of nature and humanity's peace work; both are creative processes in response to conflict. In their explanation of environmental peace, Mische and Harris (2008) explain that:

> It is an active process in which tremendous creativity is expended in an effort to balance conflicting forces and find equilibrium. It is also a process of mutual nurturance of conditions that will help sustain humans and other members of the community of life. (p. 2)

Lessons about interdependence include the emotional, spiritual, and cultural ties humans have with nature, which "interspecies communication" illustrates (Interspecies, 2014). The concepts of mutualism and ecological responsibility express interdependence for survival. Education for sustainable living in the natural environment involves social interdependence and adaption of lifestyles to avoid harm to one's surroundings (Bajaj & Chiu, 2009; Wenden, 2004). Harm that has occurred needs healing.

Repair of Harm

Harm can range in degree from minor to extreme. Destruction is extreme harm. As mentioned earlier, examination of conflict involves classification of harm. All degrees of harm are important in peace education, even though the topic of peace is most often associated with ending violence. Recognition of damage in any context calls attention to needs, especially for ways of living without harm. Small harms indicate conflict of some type that needs attention. Many conflicts begin within an individual and manifest in the communication and actions of that person. Marshall Rosenberg (2003) helps people identify the unfulfilled need, which inner and various other types of conflict reveal. His many writings, which are affordably available or cost-free from the Center for Nonviolent Communication, have aided families and teachers of youth in identifying problem sources. One tool provided for that purpose is a Feelings Inventory (Center for Nonviolent Communication, 2014). Stating one's feelings enables expression of harm done and analysis of a conflict's source. Youth and school staff learn to use a vocabulary of feelings in conflict interventions and other situations at school for description of current and possible harm.

The two types of harm-response programs developed for peace education are conflict mediation and restorative practice; both are communication-based approaches. In mediation, facilitators help disputants explain what they perceive as the conflict. If harm has been an outcome, the disputants are given an opportunity to address the conflict and the evident harm. In response to name calling, for example, or other verbal expressions that are harmful, the harmed person expresses the negative impact of the act and may suggest alternative interaction. The name caller also has an opportunity in the mediation session to explain the conflict and offer suggestions for resolving it. Restorative practices similarly involve communication between the harmer and the harmed. Optimally, community members as well as the families of those involved in the conflict participate in the restoration. With youth, repair typically involves a counseling approach to problem solving in which identity, perceptions, and needs get clarification as part of the repair process. On their website, the International Institute for Restorative Practices provides examples of "projects that use restorative solutions to solve complex social problems" (2014, para 1). In his work with restorative practices of the Maori, Cavanaugh (2009) recognized the ultimate goal to actualize what Noddings (2008) has described as caring education. A culture of care in schools has effectively incorporated compassionate communication about all types of needs, thereby avoiding escalation of conflicts to harmful outcomes (Eisler & Miller, 2004; Hart & Hodson, 2004). Caring also involves the recognition of more than the mental or physical needs of students who cope with conflict and violence. It includes liberation pedagogy that responds to disempowerment in the community of the youth and elsewhere. Lack of personal and group power to fulfill life-sustaining needs, such as access to employment, safety, and healthcare in the community, evidences political and mental harm. A government that fails to protect those who endure structural violence needs analysis of how it uses its power. Efforts to enhance humanism in political geography support student examination of power (Brunn & Yanarella, 1987).

Empowerment

In its search for the sources of problems, peace education facilitates learning about power distribution and use along with evident effects. With the goal of ending violence, peace education includes observation and description of, as well as analysis and response to, systemic conflicts such as social injustice. Access to life-sustaining resources, power to use them, and decisions about how the uses will equitably occur are the topics that prepare youth for the future and teach them to respond to current conflicts. At age-appropriate levels, they learn of issues in their neighborhood, community, and world (Evans & Saxe, 1996). Their preparation for action as members of those contexts includes sociopolitical, ethical, historical, and cultural literacies as identified in the standards for social studies education (California Department of Education, 2005). Nongovernmental organizations have been supporting development of those literacies, across subject areas and within social studies (Carter, 2013). Rethinking Schools (2014) provides publications that not only identify current power issues students have studied but also how teachers have enabled students' democratic action in response to those conflicts. These strategies, in response to power differentials, that enable students to develop multiple literacies for reading words and the world are examples of critical pedagogy.

In Brazil, Paulo Freire exemplified and then theorized education for empowerment. His last writing articulated the importance of orienting students towards ethics and civic engagement in pursuit of freedom wherever they recognize oppression (Freire, 1998). What he had in mind were human rights, which his students in Brazil lacked. By teaching them about conflict responses and developing their literacy at the same time, he provided a model that educators adopted worldwide. By elaborating on the different ways education has reproduced power imbalances, the importance of teaching youth how to recognize systemic conflicts is clear (Apple, 1995; Bourdieu & Passeron, 1977). Critical peace education incorporates this goal of preparing youth to address structural conflicts and to prevent violent responses to them (Bajaj, 2008; Snauwaert, 2011). While human and animal populations face food and safety insecurity with resulting health crises, conflict knowledge and skills are crucial in preparation for life in the future as well as the present. David Hicks points out the greater need for students involvement than learning about the problems in the world. To study only the problems, however, can be counterproductive, as research on teaching about global and future issues has shown (Hicks, 2002; Rogers, 1998).

> Students also need to explore the range of solutions that have been put into place or are being proposed for such issues. Not to do this can lead to a sense of alienation and despair. Doing this appropriately can lead to a growing sense of empowerment, and encourage the first steps in responsible global citizenship. (Hicks, 2004, p. 166)

Thinking critically about the future has been an interdisciplinary opportunity in peace education. In their case study of students studying landscapes with a critical lens for the development of peace in the future, Hutchinson and Herborn (2012) explain how there are many contexts in which to think about having a peaceable future.

Visioning

Educating toward a world without harm and violence involves picturing how a place and its inhabitants will be in the future. Creativity has been the key to developing effective conflict resolution and transformation. Elise Boulding (2000) illustrated with many accounts how societies envisioned peace to support her conclusion that "the history of nonviolence is the history of human creativity" (p. 195). The accomplishments of those who effectively counteracted structural conflicts began with a vision of a better situation for those who lacked peace. Eleanor Roosevelt envisioned children around the world with all of their life-sustaining needs fulfilled when she initiated the creation of Universal Declaration of the Human Rights by the United Nations. Samantha Smith envisioned the end of war preparations and the inimical relationship between her nation and the USSR when she reached out to Soviet Premier Yury Andropov and then the Soviet Embassy (Samantha Smith Foundation, 2014). Her work as a ten-year-old peace ambassador during the Cold War inspires children and adults to speak out about what they picture as a peaceful world. It is clear that the act of visioning has not needed a corresponding plan for manifestation of the vision. That creative work follows as the second step towards peace development. The skill of visioning is broad based and crucial.

In sites for conflict analysis, visioning also occurs. Table 1.1 offers a list of these contexts for youth to picture manifestations of peace. For example, it is crucial to think about inner conflict without a harmful response. Such activities might be contemplation or meditation to cool off emotions, art to illustrate thoughts, exploratory writing, exercise to reduce stress, and pleasurable undertakings that increase a sense of

Table 1.1 Contexts for peace visions

Site	Image of Peaceful Interaction
Inner-self	
Active-self	
Home community	
Local region	
World	
Outer space	

well-being. The image column is blank for users to create their own content.

The orientation of students towards preferable futures includes thinking about potential realities. As an aid for that process, Hutchinson (1996) offers the following questions:

> To what extent is the future narrowed to an extrapolation of existing empirical reality?
> To what extent is there is there democratic dialogue and broadened social imagination about alternative futures?
> To what extent are there practical attempts through non-violent political processes, to lessen the gap between the believed probable future and preferred alternative future? (p. 123)

These questions promote communication, analysis, and action in conjunction with visioning. A review of methods commonly used in peace education provides a more complete picture of how such instruction occurs.

Methods of Peace Education

Around the world, peace education has been taking place in several ways. This chapter describes the methods that teachers and nonformal educators in the United States, where the authors reside, have been using. There are similar, if not identical, methods used in many other regions. Some approaches to peace education exist worldwide, such as educating *for* and *about* peace.

Education For and About Peace

Teaching the capacities *for* development and preservation of peace is optimal when there is an opportunity to learn *about* how it has happened in the past as well as what thoughts and activities support those accomplishments. Betty Reardon (2000) includes these two processes in her definition of peace education.

> Peace education can be defined as: the transmission of knowledge about requirements of, the obstacles to, and possibilities for achieving and maintaining peace; training in skills for interpreting the knowledge; and the development of reflective and participatory capacities for applying the knowledge to overcome problems and achieve possibilities. (p. 399).

Youth learn both of these strands of peace education when there is stimulation of their thinking and communication about the means of peace development and the cultural contexts where those strategies occurred. In their analysis of what was done to accomplish peace, they reflect on differences and how they feel about the employed strategies. They check if the process to end violence involved harm. An awareness of values and communication behaviors aids the analysis. They consider cultural norms, like saving face versus direct blaming, in a discussion between disputants. When one disputant has a communication norm of direct eye contact and describes the problem as caused by another, they can discern differences of individualism versus collectivism or power differentials.

Positive and Negative Peace

Another universally applied method involves the evaluation of negative and positive strategies for peace. Negative peace is a term that describes the use of violence to end violence, such as war. The classification of negative peace results from the absence of compassion and creative, versus destructive, problem solving in response to existing violence. When reading literature, youth identify the presentation of negative peace and consider other possibilities for ending violence in the situation the text presents. Positive peace refers to the activities that people accomplish without harming others. While the discussions about negative and positive peace have mostly been about structural problems, which governments and societies experience, the descriptors are also useful in analysis of interactions between individuals and within the self. The internal speech of an individual who faces a conflict can be monitored as positive or negative. Developments of these thinking skills, and many other aspects of peace education, occur in several situations as a response to literature. Cross-situational learning *about* and *for* types of peace provides rich and relevant educational opportunities.

Informal Instruction

Peace education happens in many situations beyond the accomplishment of formal learning objectives that teachers make (Carter, 2004). Youth experience informal education when they observe how people think about and respond to lifestyle choices and conflicts. When adults share their thinking with youth, they can enrich the learning opportunities by providing a rationale for their response choice. Additionally, they can demonstrate dispositions that support peace. Adults can model responses that promote curiosity about and accommodation of behavioral variations in multicultural situations. Display and use of diverse cultural objects as well as visual arts provide indirect lessons on the value of diversity. Indeed, indirect methods of teaching values, through modeling, have been recognized as a more effective instruction than direct methods in which youth are told what they should think and do (Pate, 1997). Critical pedagogy involves deliberate preparation of the *hidden curriculum*, which the interactions in as well as the arrangements of the learning contexts, as comprise formal or informal education. The provision of peace literature in their homes, schools, libraries, and spirituality sites where youth interact with texts is an example of hidden curriculum. It becomes formal instruction when planned lessons incorporate the use of that literature.

Formal Instruction

Facilitation of formal instruction happens in the enactment of learning objectives that educators, in schools and other organizations, plan for optimal learning opportunities. Although the description here of trends in formal instruction at schools does not describe the support that other organizations provide, there is no intention of diminishing their importance. All sites of formal education that support peace competencies can augment learning by youth. Certainly, identification and analysis of conflict sources and responses to them need to happen across the life circumstances of youth. Clarification of the approaches to peace education in schools can stimulate awareness of possibilities for use of these methods in other circumstances of formal education.

Table 1.2 lists formal instruction characterized by multiple components. Here, the presentation of these components is

Table 1.2 Pedagogy of peace education

Component	Enactment
Holistic	Incorporation of aesthetics and all dimensions of the individual, including body, mind, emotions, and spirituality
Contextual	Responsive to current conditions
Community based	Interaction with community members, school partnerships with community members, and global connection
Sensitizing	Awareness of others' perceptions and needs
Powerful	Meaningful, integrative, value-based, challenging, and active
Critical	Higher-level thinking about relationships and conflict sources
Narrow to broad	Roots and extent of conflict

brief because subsequent chapters elaborate on their facilitation with literature.

In holistic instruction, youth connect many aspects of their lives to the learning topic. They are shown the wholeness of their lives in relation to peace and how to experience it through their senses (Montessori, 1992; Seldin, 1999). Some of the theorists who contributed to holistic pedagogy were Pestalozzi, Thoreau, Montessori, and Steiner (Miller, 1991). The community orientation of peace education builds on the experiential approach by involving members of the local and global community, as they are available for communication with the youth (Eisler, 2000; Maguth & Hilburn, 2011). The National Council for the Social Studies (2014) articulated strands of powerful instruction. Meaningful learning happens when there is depth of learning about a concept. That involves incorporation of student schema, or background, including existing knowledge and experiences. Integrative instruction coherently combines disciplines that are otherwise separated as distinct subject areas (Brunson, Conte, & Masar, 2002; Carter, 2003/2010; Ndura-Quédraogo & Amster, 2009). Value-based lessons engage learners in the identification of evident values and development of those that support peace, such as concern for others, empathy, respect, trust, and equality. Instruction that is challenging provides learners with opportunities for in-depth inquiry and clarity in articulating a proposed response that derives from analysis of the content studied. Completing the construal of powerful teaching is active learning, whereby students do something to develop their knowledge and skills, like the use of their physical capacities as well as their minds in response to a problem. Expanding on that notion is critical thinking, which involves analysis, synthesis, and evaluation of the information the learning opportunity presents.

The context of peace education influences the substance and the form of the purposeful lessons. The intended contents, versus those that result from student inquiry, derive from directives for student learning and the hidden curriculum, such as what has been excluded as topics and skills that are relevant to peace development. The second aspect of contextual instruction is the form of peace education. Johan Galtung emphasizes that the sources of structural conflict, which critical examination of them evidences, need to be transformed into learning sites of peace. He calls for exemplification of peace within the institution through the means they provide for learning (2004). That indicates the facilitators of the informal as well as formal lessons in the schools must demonstrate peace through their modeling of knowledge, skills, and dispositions. Additionally, Galtung explains that learning needs to be student-centered with accommodation of their learning interests as well as their schema and cultural norms. Optimally, peace education is comprehensive and responsive to current conditions of humanity and other life forms in the world. The narrow-to-broad approach facilitates identification of conflict sources along with their effects, all of which need consideration and appropriate responses.

Rationale for Peace Education with Youth Literature

Rationale for instruction with literature includes tradition, bonding through enjoyment, in addition to usability for development of language and visual skills. First, storytelling is a long human tradition in which literature continues for continuity in education. Before print versions, and subsequent to that means for sharing many stories, oral traditions around the world included presentation and illustration of peace-related concepts and skills. Music was another way of passing on that information, as well as stimulating action in response to conflict. The usability of story in text and other formats fit well in the education of youth because it stimulates both language development and lessons relative to many aspects of life, which are now separated disciplines of study. Language development occurs through listening to or reading text, of any type. Hence, the language forms that support peace can be indirectly taught through the engagement of youth with literature that features such discourse. Applied peace linguistics is a descriptor for language forms and uses that support peace-oriented communication (Crystal, 2001; Gomes de Matos, 2003). The discourse in the text and the images it provides to represent the characters, as well as the strategies they use in response to conflict, are rich resources for indirect and direct instruction. The situations, in which adults facilitate the uses of literature to teach, or just be together, are bonding opportunities. These facets of using literature in peace education all support reading to and by youth as informal as well as formal instruction.

Literature provides instructional contents and a means for curriculum integration. The discourse and graphic presentations of literature feature substance for thinking about the underlying sources of conflict and violence. Analysis of the literature's discourse style involves identification of how it expresses ideologies, identities, interactions, and illustrations of values that support or undermine peace. Graphic features of the text accomplish the same through layout along with setting, character, and plot representations. The concepts the literature presents, across languages and within them that are nontransliteral, are especially salient in texts that youth enjoy. The attraction to continued use of the literature increases learning potential. Translation across languages of the same text adds to opportunities for knowledge and skill acquisition, while it also expresses pluralism. Definitely, good literature offers many competencies of social education.

Social Literacy

Social literacy refers to the linguistic, psychological, cultural, political, and ethical aspects of human interaction. "Social literacy is concerned with the empowerment of the social and ethical self which includes the ability to understand and explain differences within individual experiences" (Arthur & Davison, 2000, p.14). Another aspect of social literacy is how youth will understand their rights in a society and their duty to benefit that collective. The tension sometimes lies between individual and social benefits, when there is a conflict between the two that is apparent to youth.

Literacy in the social realm of life is a universal goal for youth. Evidence of social intelligence can be identified in the ways that people shape, as well as fit into, their cultures and positively interact with others who have cultural differences. The rationale for social literacy exists across disciplines as well as in the society that expects its youth to at least sustain its future survival, if not accomplish peacemaking where direct violence is present (McGlynn, Zembylas, Bekerman, & Gallagher, 2009). Social literacy develops from learning in all subject and skill areas that include human interactions. The decisions people have made and their corresponding behaviors are foci of social literacy. Hence, how people have made decisions that contributed to peace is content for learning in each subject area that schools provide (Hall, 1993). Worldwide, there has been a range of standards and guidelines across subject areas and other aspects of formal education to recommend instruction that supports social literacy. Peace educators are responsive to the standards-driven education (Carter, 2008).

Summary

This chapter described facets of peace education, an orientation for instruction across the curriculum in literacy and social education. It reviewed the construal of peace across world regions that include harmonious living, conflict prevention, avoidance and repair of harm, fulfillment of needs, as well as social and legal justice. The context of a society determines how people conceive of peace and teach for its maintenance and development. Instruction incorporates informal and formal lessons about conflict, coexistence, sustainable living, repair of harm, empowerment, and envisioning peace. The rationale for instruction with literature includes tradition, usability, language and visual content, bonding through enjoyment, and curriculum integration. Social literacy is a universal goal for youth that peace education pursues through use of literature.

2
Characterization

Character development and situation in the plot, including the social context of a story, are factors that shape readers' perceptions. Presentation of characters can perpetuate myths of otherness and stimulate feelings of fear as well as distrust. However, characters may be presented in ways that make commonalities apparent and promote positive perceptions, laying the foundation for mutually respectful relationships. This chapter addresses and discusses examples of characters and characterization in stories that affect readers' perceptions of self and others, along with ways people respond to conflict.

Construal of Peace

According to Danesh and Clarke-Habibi (2007), individuals interpret the nature of reality through worldviews that are shaped by how we perceive ourselves, others, interactions, and possibilities. Various unique and shared experiences shape and reshape our worldviews. In particular, children's experiences with literature in formal and informal learning situations contribute to shaping their worldviews of individuals, groups, and societies. To varying degrees, children are exposed to violence through media and personal experience. As a result of that exposure, a belief that violence is normal can affect their worldviews. It is essential to teach children about peaceful ways of being to counter the often unexamined messages that promote acceptance of violence as inevitable—to introduce a vision of peace so children can critique and understand conditions that promote harmonious living as well as those that produce conflict.

Selecting books to use for teaching peace is a serious matter that requires careful consideration of the messages, both explicit and implicit, that stories convey. The first chapter of this book discussed harmonious living, conflict prevention, avoidance and repair of harm, fulfillment of needs in addition to social and legal justice as aspects of peace. These concepts provide a useful framework to begin thinking about messages that the characters' experiences, perceptions, and behaviors can convey.

Good stories have the potential to influence the way children think about how the world works, their own lives, and relationships with others at both conscious and subconscious levels. Through the vicarious experiences of characters, readers may become aware of possibilities for living peacefully as they come to understand the complexity of conflict and potential responses to it. However, simply recognizing and understanding the causes of conflict is not enough. Living peacefully requires the knowledge and skills to prevent conflict when possible, resolve conflict without violence, and repair harm caused by injustice and conflict. Stories demonstrating the sources, prevention, and resolution of conflict, along with the importance of repairing harm, help to expand and inform readers' worldviews and actions. When readers make personal connections, when they care about the characters in stories, these vicarious experiences naturally influence worldviews by adding to their lived experience.

Using youth literature to teach is an example of a narrow-to-broad approach to peace education that allows readers to make text-to-self and text-to-world connections. This occurs when children encounter engaging characters and have opportunities to grapple with difficult issues in relatively low-risk venues, such as literature study groups, recreating stories through drama, and journaling. Those personal experiences, within the safe space of a book, allow readers to build a foundation for developing understandings and responses that are essential for caring and peaceful ways of being.

Harmonious Living

The Merriam-Webster Online Dictionary (2012) defines the term *harmonious* as "having the parts agreeably related." For diverse groups and individuals to relate agreeably is challenging, given that the variety of life experiences represented on the planet shapes worldviews that are often incongruent and perceived to be in conflict. It implies awareness and understanding that, while everyone has common needs, diverse ways of meeting them vary according to cultural norms, thus shaping wide-ranging perspectives of lived differences. To relate agreeably requires mutual understanding of dissimilar perspectives and the forces that shaped them, along with the skills and processes needed for peaceable interactions between and within groups.

Harmonious living differs from societal order maintained through force and domination. A foundation for harmonious living allows much conflict to be avoided when relationships and the social contract are based on recognition of inherent human dignity and worth, and an understanding that social justice can be achieved only when opportunities for fulfilling needs are equitable through shared power and responsibility. Conflict is further avoided when legal justice formally reinforces that social contract and serves to protect those opportunities for all. Within that caring framework, conflict becomes an opportunity for positive action—to respond to conflict and injustice with an orientation toward repairing harm and finding a solution for meeting needs rather than as a stimulus for violence. These concepts are complex and often controversial, yet it is possible for young people to become aware of sensitive social issues and learn to think critically and creatively when they encounter engaging characters and experiences to which they can relate in quality literature.

Since literary plots often revolve around problems and resolutions, the very structure of a story makes youth literature a particularly useful method for presenting characters with a spectrum of life experiences and differing worldviews who demonstrate caring, solution-oriented perspectives and action. As with children's literature in general, the element of characterization is important when selecting quality texts. Specific character traits, behaviors, and contexts are critical factors to consider when selecting literature to teach children about peace and harmonious living. Through characters, readers have opportunities to meet people who have varying experiences, cultures, abilities, and appearances, and yet share their most basic needs and values. Readers alter their worldviews when introduced to characters that are different from the people they encounter in daily life; thus, they make inferences about real people from the characters they meet in stories. As they come to know characters through stories, readers are able to see beyond differences and stereotypes. While they come to know characters as individuals, readers have the opportunity to become aware of the common threads within humanity. Likewise, as readers share the characters' experiences, social justice issues may be revealed in ways that enable them to relate and care about the consequences of inequity and injustice.

Characters and Peace Education

Peace education aims to "make the world a better, more humane place" by addressing real problems and promoting justice, equality, and tolerance (Bar-Tal, 2002, p. 28). Elements of character and characterization that promote justice, equality, and tolerance in the face of real problems are important to consider when using literature in peace education. Books have the capacity to introduce readers to people with varying experiences, cultures, abilities, and appearances in both familiar and unfamiliar situations (Levin, 2007).

Thankfully, children's literature with diverse characters is much more readily available today than it was when Nancy Larrick announced in *The All-White World of Children's Books* (1965) that less than 1 percent of all books published for children represented African Americans in contemporary settings. While Larrick focused on the specific representation of African Americans, other nondominant groups have also been underrepresented in children's literature. While these groups are still underrepresented, increased publication of books representing diversity has subsequently been a positive trend. This greater availability of choice makes it possible to consider quality when selecting books for use with young people (Braus & Geidel, 2000; Emery, 2003).

Even as we seek to include material that provides a range of diverse characters and addresses social issues, as educators we must be critical in our analyses of these texts to ensure that the books we use do not reinforce stereotypes or promote conflict. The ways in which characters are developed and situated in both the plot and social context of the story play important roles in determining how readers will perceive them. Characters presented in ways that perpetuate a myth of otherness may perhaps stimulate unexamined feelings of fear and distrust. However, characters presented in ways that make commonalities apparent may promote positive perceptions, laying the foundation for mutually respectful relationships.

In her landmark book, *Black History in the Pages of Children's Literature*, Casement (2008) demonstrates the power of literature in promoting critical thinking and mutual understanding by presenting significant works that reflect a rich history of African Americans from pre-Colonial through contemporary times. She makes it very clear that "...no major event in America's history could be authentically represented without the inclusion of African Americans who were here every day in every way as part of the drama of our nation's history" (p. v). However, this information is hardly included in history textbooks, leaving most citizens unaware of the continual contributions of and challenges faced by African Americans throughout the centuries. Through compelling stories, Casement's readers meet historical and fictional characters. Awareness of those experiences replaces stereotypes. When sharing experiences and events with characters set in this historical context, readers become aware of the effects of prejudice and discrimination, along with the significance and power of relationships in defining social and legal justice and injustice. Through stories, the influence of those often abstract issues on the lives of individuals and groups of people become real and heartfelt. This approach inspires empathy, caring, and desire for positive change.

The works presented in Casement's book tell stories that may inspire newfound respect and admiration for the lives of untold African Americans in history. At the same time, many tell powerful stories of tragedy, suffering, and injustice that may inspire feelings of great sadness or outrage. As such, it is important to note that merely reading these stories is not enough. Youth need question and discussion interactions after reading. Therefore, the guidance of adults willing to listen is essential for youth to confront their feelings and posit responses.

Diversity in Main and Supporting Characters

A key consideration when using youth literature is in the representation of diversity. The ways characters represent factors such as age, culture, gender, abilities, religion, region, social class, language, race, and ethnicity will influence whether they reinforce stereotypes or foster respect and understanding. It is important that stories represent main characters, particularly protagonists, from a variety of different backgrounds, within settings and situations to which readers can relate. Gail Tompkins (2007) writes, "Inferring a character's traits is an important part of reading" (p. 234). The information at hand, along with readers' own worldviews and prior knowledge, influence the inferences they make. Authors develop character traits as they write about appearance, action, dialogue, and monologue. This gives readers insight into a character's feelings, perceptions, and motives. When authors provide more information about a character, readers rely less on their personal experiences for interpreting text. Portraying unique aspects of the main character's perspective and culture within universal sorts of experiences can help readers cross cultural borders and foster understanding and respect (Banks, 1997).

While presenting stories that encompass themes familiar to readers, the perspectives, attitudes, and feelings of the represented groups should accurately portray the unique ways that people express universal feelings and meet common needs. Because main characters are more fully developed than supporting characters, readers get to know them better and tend to interpret the story from that character's point of view. It follows that readers, through coming to understand and know the main characters, are able to make connections that are more personal. They are then able to relate to the needs, experiences, and feelings of characters that are different from their own (e.g., race, gender, religion, nationality, ability). Those vicarious experiences allow readers to consider multiple perspectives and recognize commonalities; as a result, differences become less threatening. However, authors provide less information about supporting characters, so readers naturally rely on their personal experiences and worldviews when forming perceptions of character traits. Thus, readers may unwittingly rely upon stereotypes when they come across supporting characters from groups with whom they have little personal knowledge. In addition, supporting characters generally elicit less conscious analysis, leaving open the possibility that stereotypes are not challenged but instead reinforced.

As children begin to learn about self and others during their early years, they become very aware of difference (Biles, 1994; Connolly, Smith, & Kelly, 2002; Derman-Sparks & Edwards, 2010). As they continue to experience new things and people, they develop mental maps or schemas to organize their understanding of the world, developing categories and hierarchies (Piaget, 1952). These schemas may be organized in ways that define different types of people as good or bad, strong or weak, lazy or hardworking, smart or foolish, safe or frightening; this is largely determined by social interactions (Vygotsky, 1978) and societal messages, including media and literature.

When children are exposed to literature that repeatedly depicts people from certain groups as the main characters, with other groups only seen in supporting roles, this may plant seeds for believing that some groups of people are more important than others. Readers' perceptions of power and status are affected by who they see as being the most important people in the story. This is important to note when using literature to teach for peace and justice because in the world of literature, even with the progress made, the representation among all people is still unequal in the roles of main characters. While now more than ever, children's literature does represent diversity, there is still far to go before the world represented in books matches the real world experienced by the children. Unless adults consciously expose children to a wide variety of literature, with strong and diverse types of characters accurately portrayed, we may unwittingly promote bias.

Likewise, we might unintentionally reinforce stereotypes when we attempt to provide an array of literature with single representations of different groups to introduce a broad range of diversity. Selecting and engaging in a variety of books that represent different and contemporary experiences across and within groups is necessary to avoid reinforcing stereotypes.

Although a single book might be an accurate representation of a segment of a culture, ethnicity, region, or ability group, if children experience only that one book, they will have a limited perspective of that group. Brashears (2012) explains that the book *When I Was Young in the Mountains* (Rylant, 1982) is a historically accurate portrayal of the life of a loving Appalachian family. However, it does not reflect the complexity of the lives and experiences across Appalachia, nor does it represent changes that have occurred over time. Without exposure to information reflecting a range of Appalachian experiences, children may form very narrow and inaccurate understandings of people who live in that region.

Similarly, *Going Home* (Bunting, 1996) tells the story of a loving family that has emigrated from Mexico to work gathering crops in California and returns to their home village for a visit. Their story represents the hard work and sacrifices made by loving parents to ensure opportunity and a better life for their children. While this is a universal theme and the characters are realistic, powerful, and engaging, this book alone gives readers a narrow view of the diverse roles, backgrounds, and careers of Mexican people. For children to develop an understanding of the range of diversity within groups of people, they must engage with a variety of texts to meet unique individuals in various contexts.

While mental maps and worldviews continue to change throughout life, foundations for respect or bias can be established early on, and subsequent experiences will either reinforce or challenge previous notions. Therefore, it is critical to consider the quality and presentation of characters' messages in texts from the earliest experiences throughout childhood. Caring adults who guide discussion and questioning with children are necessary to help children consider the unfamiliar and deconstruct stereotypes and biases.

Finally, regardless of personal life experiences, ongoing depictions of certain types of people in dominant roles will lead to a perception that some groups are more important and better than others. It is illustrated and reinforced that everyone has value when characters from different backgrounds join together to solve problems and work for mutual goals. The underlying message defines common humanity and demonstrates the importance of collaboration for the good of all. There is an urgent need for this message to counter and reshape a worldview that demonizes the "other" as the source of a problem and promotes violent conflict.

Fulfillment of Needs and Responding to Conflict

Characters who act in ways that dominate or are hurtful to others to meet their own needs when feeling anger, loneliness, jealousy, or fear demonstrate violence as a conflict response. However, the same characters might model peaceful responses as they act autonomously to meet the needs causing those feelings. In doing so, characters can inspire readers and promote prosocial thinking and acting.

Say Something (Moss, 2004) begins with the line, "There's a kid in my school who gets picked on all the time." On subsequent pages the protagonist, a schoolgirl, introduces the reader to other children who are teased. She describes the children's responses to the teasing and states that she feels sorry for them. However, she does nothing when she witnesses it but points out that she's not a bullying participant. When she becomes the victim of teasing, her perception changes. She then describes her own pain, shame, and anger at the children who watch but do not help her. The plot of this story is familiar to readers, who will likely identify with the role of at least one of the characters. The story ends simply, but powerfully, when the protagonist sits on the bus next to the girl who had always been sitting alone and realizes that the girl is "really funny." This realization is important because it makes clear that the girl who always sits alone is a person of value, perhaps a friend—in any case, not simply a victim in need of protection. When she reaches out to another, the protagonist models a solution that not only avoids conflict through collaboration but also finds a way to repair harm when she realizes that she had been part of the problem through her own inaction. The protagonist expresses strong feelings and models a response to her own anger at the violence of bullying by reaching out to another. The awareness that she is not perfect is an important aspect of her to which all readers may relate. This character's experiences and actions are a highly relatable example of how an individual can transform a problem to make a positive contribution.

The visual representation of characters is important as well. The illustrations of characters in *Say Something* (Moss, 2004) depict many types of diversity, including race, ability, and gender. Since members from different groups are both the perpetrators and victims of bullying behaviors, the author guides readers away from a view that only certain types of people are bullies. Instead, teasing is seen as a human problem and actively caring about each other is offered as a solution.

With guidance from an adult, this book can stimulate reflection on their own experiences, develop empathy, recognize bullying as violence and develop proactive responses that promote personal and group solutions. Actions that cause harm to others stem from attempts to fulfill unmet needs like safety, belonging, esteem, and access to resources (Fields, Perry, & Fields, 2009; Gartrell, 2006). It is important to explore potential sources of bullying behaviors instead of labeling a bully as a bad person who must be defeated. Characters allow readers to consider the reasons for and responses to bullying without the risks involved in the realities that youth face. While reading, discussing, and analyzing the possible unmet needs that may be sources of hurtful behaviors, youth can contribute to developing strategies to prevent this type of conflict.

For example, in *Bridge to Terabithia* (Patterson, 1977) the notorious bully, Janice Avery, is a victim of child abuse. In the beginning, the protagonists, Jesse and Leslie, feel anger and fear toward Janice. They cannot overpower her physically. So in retribution for the bullying, they trick her, and the trick causes Janice emotional suffering and humiliation. As creative and intelligent children, it is possible they could overpower Janice through psychological strategies. However, they become aware of Janice's own suffering from abuse and respond with compassion. When they find that she is a human being with similar needs, they no longer react to her with fear. Since the school bully is a virtual archetype throughout time and place, the context of this story provides a venue for readers to connect their own experiences in the larger world to the problems faced by its characters. Jesse and Leslie's initial responses to a frightening bully and their reflections on their own actions offer room for a critical analysis and discussion of positive peace—as a condition where the needs of all are considered, compassion is felt and communication is used to achieve solutions. In contrast is the condition of negative peace, where the needs of some are sacrificed and order is kept by exerting power over others.

Empowerment and Social Justice

In *The Other Side* (2001), Jacqueline Woodson tells a story that demonstrates the power to influence change through personal, autonomous acts. Two young girls, one black and one white, challenge the social order when they sit together on a fence that clearly divides their town according to race. At first, although they become friends, neither risks venturing to "the other side." Both have been warned by their mothers that it isn't safe to cross the boundary. They respond in use of the fence that kept them apart. The very symbol of division becomes the place to connect and communicate. The friendship grows and the girls leave us with a message: "Someday somebody's going to come along and knock this old fence down." As a potent story of friendship, children will naturally question the whys. Why was the fence there? Why was segregation the law? Why did the girls believe that it was dangerous to cross? Perhaps some children will question why we are still so separated. With these questions opportunities abound to critically examine beliefs and policies that foster separatism, along with possibilities to come together.

Christopher Paul Curtis brings compelling characters to life in his books for older elementary through adolescent children. The stories are told from the perspectives of African American children with talents and challenges, who experience joy and despair, love and loneliness, courage and fear, resilience and humor. In his book *The Mighty Miss Malone* (2012), Deza's feelings, needs, and experiences as a child growing up during the Great Depression represent themes of a time that crosses cultural boundaries.

When tragedy forces her family to leave their home and go on the road, we share the perils of traveling the rails. We learn that the hobos who surreptitiously rode in train cars were often families with children who risked their lives in desperation. When her family stumbles upon a "Hooverville" community, readers experience a very real example of conflict transformation when strangers choose to cooperate in desperate circumstances. In Hoovervilles throughout the United States, destitute people gathered outside cities for protection and to share their meager resources. Rather than harming others in competition for food and shelter, they came together out of necessity to support one another in efforts to meet common needs for survival. Through Deza, readers experience the brutality of law enforcement officials toward the homeless families and individuals who were residents of a Hooverville, as well as the fear and sense of helplessness that was so common during that time. Still, the actions of Deza and others in the group demonstrate the power of individuals to survive in trying times without resorting to violent conflict. Within Deza's deeply personal experience, readers learn a bit of history and become aware of the societal conditions and laws that undermined survival activities of the very poor.

Clearly, suffering was a reality for all sorts of people during that time. Still, Curtis sets the story solidly within the experiences of a Midwestern African American family in the 1930s, and the realities of racism are part of the larger story. Deza is a bright, precocious, and personable child. Her family is honorable and hardworking. In spite of their strengths, Deza and her family face hardship and uncertainty. Through this captivating story and its characters' experiences, all readers feel the effects of societal racism and inequality as personal and unjust, while at the same time recognizing common humanity along with the strengths and values of the African American community that enable individuals to persevere.

Christopher Curtis's books are examples of the power youth literature holds in telling enjoyable stories while presenting uncomfortable realities from unique perspectives that relate to readers from all walks of life. For teachers and parents, these books provide opportunities to promote critical thinking and social consciousness without promoting defensiveness or division. Even as the stories realistically portray hardship, they also portray kindness and caring behaviors among strangers as well as loved ones. In the characters' eyes, readers confront issues of poverty, racism, and injustice while experiencing the effects of related social policies. Through their struggles and triumphs, Deza and her family demonstrate the power of love and determination while they demonstrate moral autonomy.

Conflict Prevention and Repair of Harm

Considering how characters behave in solving problems is as important as the character representation of who solves the problem. When characters achieve their goals through force or harm to others, this reinforces a message that violent solutions are justified. Young people are exposed to a steady diet of violence through the media and, in many cases, through personal experiences—sometimes to the point that violent behaviors may seem natural. Carefully selecting literature that depicts alternatives to violence in familiar situations provides opportunities to help children recognize violence and learn strategies for peaceful action. The selection and use of the text must be intentional and explicit to counter the continuous, subtle, and not-so-subtle messages that suggest violence is inevitable.

Because the resolution of problems is important to storytelling, literature implicitly teaches readers about peace and violence in a variety of ways. Stories might reinforce or redefine traditional power structures, depending upon which characters have the problem and which characters solve the problem. Young people can be empowered and learn from the behaviors of characters that come up with solutions individually or in collaboration with others. Or, they might learn they are vulnerable and dependent on assistance from others that are more powerful. When readers experience young people working together or with adults to solve problems, they may develop a sense of agency. Likewise, when readers encounter characters representing strong women, strong members of diverse ethnic groups, and strong people with physical challenges as individuals with the feelings, ideas, and skills needed to solve problems, their worldviews may expand to include all people as valuable and potential partners.

While good versus evil is a popular story line, in reality, conflict is much more complex than mere dichotomy. Helping children to understand the contexts for characters' behaviors promotes their understanding of common needs and multiple sources of conflict.

Barbara Joosse (2002) broaches the subject of gang violence in *Star in the Darkness*. She tells the story of a family struggling to survive the poverty and violence of their neighborhood. Told from the perspective of his little brother, it tells the story of Richard, who becomes a banger, believing it is the only way to make money and keep them safe. Although Richard tries to keep it a secret, Mama and little brother "know what they know." They realize that Richard is in a gang, but know he is still good on the inside because he loves them and takes care of them. They begin to believe that the other gang members might have some good inside of them too. So they come up with a plan and talk with the neighbors. The families join together and hold hands as they walk with flashlights in nightly peace walks on the streets to discourage shooting and killing. They are still afraid, the gangs still exist, but together they have hope.

Star in the Darkness does not propose a simple solution to a complex problem, but it does tell a story of empowerment and hope for change. The community demonstrates a response to the fear of violence that is very different from one of getting bigger guns and shooting first. This book has to be used carefully, with guided discussion that allows children to express their fears, confront stereotypes, explore underlying causes, and consider solutions. Guiding and engaging youth in reflection and critical discussions is essential for the effective use of literature in teaching about peace. Whether the resolution of conflict in stories meets the needs of others, as well as those of the protagonists, is an important question that will most likely have challenging answers.

Allowing children to consider characters in their entirety, flaws and all, is much more useful in developing skills and dispositions to live peaceably than defining heroes and villains. When perfect or magical characters solve problems, it may be difficult for readers to relate or make connections to how their own actions can create positive change. Furthermore, when characters are realistic human beings, winning will be an unacceptable solution if it causes pain or suffering to others. Somehow, violent action is accepted as justified when the targets are characters that are simply defined as evil. Likewise, exploring whether characters demonstrated problems solved through power over others or power to work with others to achieve change (Wasserman, 2000) is a way to engage children in learning to discriminate between behaviors that are empowered and morally autonomous from those that seek to dominate others.

Believable characters are not those that are perfect but rather those who express the same range of emotions and needs that the readers experience. Such characters provide positive models for morally autonomous behaviors and counter the notion that a superhero with special powers is necessary to solve problems. Believable characters promote empowerment and the belief that everyone can make a difference.

A superhero does not come to the rescue when children are bullied in *Say Something* (Moss, 2004), and Mama does not buy a gun for protection in *Stars in the Darkness* (Joosse, 2002). Instead, the characters in both stories take small, yet courageous, actions for positive change. Without violent action or superhero characters, both stories are engaging with realistic characters that have real feelings and respond to complex problems with well thought-out actions.

Guided discussions about the characters' behaviors can help young people who are accustomed to the good-guy or bad-guy scenarios recognize that ordinary people can act for positive change. Encountering and discussing stories that address meaningful situations can empower youth with broader perspectives and strategies for peaceful responses to conflict in their own lives.

Questions to Consider for Characterization in Youth Literature

From Evaluation Criteria for Youth Literature in Peace Education

Copyright Candice C. Carter and Shelly Clay-Robison

1. Are the characters believable?
2. Do characters reinforce societal (i.e., gender, cultural, economic) stereotypes?
3. Do characters that collaborate in the stories come from different backgrounds?

4. Which characters have the problem, and who is solving these conflicts?
5. Do characterizations reinforce typical power structures?
6. Do characters behave in ways that relate to the fulfillment of needs?
7. Do characters' responses to conflict promote fulfilling needs of the self and others?
8. Do characters model avoidance and repair of harm?
9. Can the readers identify with the characters?

Summary

In summary, social interactions, including engagement with texts, can have a profound effect on developing worldviews. As outlooks vary widely and often seem to be in conflict, it is essential that youth consider multiple perspectives and experiences for mutually respectful relationships with a range of diverse people. Literature can be a valuable resource for teaching peace when the balance of books selected represents diverse experiences, realities, and perspectives, and the characters act as models for caring behaviors and peaceful responses to conflict. Equally with high-quality literature are the environments and opportunities that encourage youth as they question, discuss, and respond to issues they encounter in literature.

3
Diversity

The *Illustrated Oxford Dictionary* (2003) simply defines diverse as "unlike in nature or qualities; varied." As such, diversity is a wide-ranging and all encompassing concept that is an essential aspect of life and social organization at all levels. The spectrum of variations in the human experience enriches life and offers a wealth of resources for meeting challenges and solving problems with a myriad of perspectives, experiences, skills, and talents. Still, differences among people are often a source of misunderstandings, fear, and prejudice that lead to conflict and difference, which are too often used to justify exclusion, oppression, and exploitation. Clearly, peace is not possible without mutual understanding, respect, and equity for all. Youth literature is an effective venue for learning about diversity in ways that foster understanding, esteem, and empathy. In this chapter we discuss aspects of diversity related to peace and present examples of literature for youth that can be used to foster understanding.

Construal of Peace

Diversity is necessary for life, yet that very necessity is often unacknowledged. Too often, human differences are defined to create social hierarchies that promote separation and undermine understanding. Peace education includes opportunities to cross the boundaries of social division and develop mutual understanding and respect.

The field of multicultural education provides a useful framework for thinking about diversity in relation to peace. The National Association for Multicultural Education (NAME) articulates a philosophy of inclusion based on *freedom, justice, equity, and human dignity*. Multicultural education goals of inclusion, equity of educational opportunity, culturally responsive content and practice, addressing social justice, all align with the construal of peace. Beyond learning to value difference and recognize injustice, multicultural education aims to foster transformative thinking and working for positive change in prosocial ways (Banks & McGee, 2008; Simone & Norton, 2011).

Children's literature can be used to address diversity and social justice issues through all genres. Picture books, novels, biographies, poetry, and expository text promote positive self-concepts and appreciation for all children by representing diverse groups (Steiner, 2008). Stories told through youth literature can help children of all backgrounds make connections to their own lives. Inclusive stories encourage respect and acceptance as they become aware of a range of diverse lived experiences (Colby & Lyon, 2004; Pires, 2011). Exposure to a variety of high-quality literature offers insights that allow children to recognize that everyone has unique and valuable characteristics, ideas, and skills that contribute to the well-being of the whole (Morgan, 2009; Simon & Norton, 2011).

Many books respond to young children's interest and curiosity about self and others by depicting common experiences. *The Milestones Project: Celebrating Children Around the World* (Steckel & Steckel, 2007), for example, introduces the reader to children from around the world through photographs and interviews. Children share feelings and milestones that are common to children far and wide, but depict differences in abilities, interests, and social contexts.

Inclusive contemporary and historical literature presents the challenges and contributions of people from groups that have been underrepresented. *Black Heroes: Scientists, Healers and Inventors* (Hudson, 2003), *Extraordinary Girls* (Ajmera, Omolodun, & Strunk, 2000), *Stories from the Silk Road* (Gilchrist, 2005), and *Home to Medicine Mountain* (Santiago & Lowrey, 1998) are examples of books that present a range of experiences and demonstrate the positive contributions from diverse people. Increased awareness cultivates an appreciation of others and challenges stereotypes. As authentic literature tells the stories of people from diverse backgrounds, the difficulties caused by discrimination are revealed to the reader. As readers relate to the characters, they are able to empathize with victims of bias and oppression, which lays a foundation for caring and thinking critically about and responding to social justice issues.

Access to knowledge is essential to meeting basic needs and participating fully in society. Thus, using inclusive children's literature contributes to social justice by fostering an optimal environment for successful learning by all children. Offering literature that depicts student's experiences and cultures, communicates that they are valued and reinforces positive self-concepts (Bynoe, 2004). Literature that engages youth with relevant issues, questions, and problems allows for meaningful engagement in academic activities (Freire, 1990; Nieto, 2000). In short, educational experiences that embrace and reflect the lives of students provide opportunities for successful learning, while exclusion from the curriculum puts students at a disadvantage (Darder, 2012).

Anti-bias education is a critical component of peace education (Levin, 2010). From an early age, children notice and use differences to develop concepts and theories for understanding the world (Connolly, Smithy, & Kelly, 2002; Piaget, 1952). Personal experiences and social interactions influence how children interpret and define difference to construct personal and social identities. (Copple & Bredekamp, 2009; Vygotsky, 1978). Media, observations, and responses to their questions and theories all influence theories that they develop about diversity (Van Ausdale & Feagin, 2001). Thus, whether children respond to difference with fear and hate, or with acceptance and appreciation is largely dependent upon the social context that they experience (Derman-Sparks & Edwards, 2010; Levin, 2010).

Children, too often, receive implicit and explicit messages of social bias before they are able to recognize or critically assess them (Lantieri & Patti, 1996). When that happens, those biases influence the theories children develop about themselves and others. Fortunately, children's natural curiosity is a boundless source of teachable moments for countering biased cultural messages that might otherwise be internalized as unexamined prejudices.

Role of Youth Literature

High-quality youth literature provides opportunities for adults to respond to children's natural curiosity. Reading inclusive literature and talking with children can validate their observations and questions in order to frame diversity in a positive light. Positive representations allow children to identify and counter stereotypes to increase understanding and respect.

Books for youth represent a spectrum of diversity. Very young children are especially interested in the observable differences related to individuals and families. Picture books effectively portray visible differences in appearance and experience within universally understood concepts. Family, for example, is a concept that is central to all children and represents love, belonging, safety, and caring for each other. Yet, there are many different configurations of families and ways of living. Diverse families can be represented in the context of good stories. For example, *Pablo's Tree* (Mora, 1994) portrays adoption within the story of a grandfather's loving tradition of planting trees in honor of grandchildren, and *Daddy, Papa and Me* (Newman, 2005) depicts the fun-filled day of a toddler and his two dads. Families are the main theme for other books like *Families are Special* (Simon,

2003) that are written specifically to promote awareness and appreciation for difference.

Older children are able to consider increasingly complex ideas about diversity. Youth literature can provide sensitive and comprehensive views of a range of living conditions and, at the same time, highlight strengths that characterize individuals, families, and groups in all types of situations. Realistic portrayals allow children to see beyond stereotypes and encourage critical thinking. For example, Francisco Jimenez tells the story of his childhood in *The Circuit: Stories from the Life of a Migrant Child* (1997) to reveal the love, hard work, and dedication that allowed his family to persevere through trying times. The story highlights positive attributes while it conveys the struggles of immigration and hardships of life as migrant farm workers through family narrative.

Harmonious Living

Living together can be quite challenging for people with varying worldviews and life experiences. Individuals and groups must be able to understand the perspectives and experiences of others in order to attain the respect, trust, and cooperation that are foundations for living in harmony. Stories allow readers to make personal connections to characters in a variety of social contexts that give meaning to perspectives and ways of living that may differ from their own (Gilligan, 1982; Morgan, 2009; Perini, 2002). Those vicarious experiences can lead to understanding, respect, and dispositions toward cooperation and helping others. In an era when competition characterizes dominant culture, carefully chosen literature can introduce the benefits of cooperative approaches to living.

Literature provides examples for youth of all ages. For the very young, *The Little Red Pen* (Stevens, 2011) extends the basic plot line of the classic folk tale, *The Little Red Hen,* to show the benefits of helping and cooperation. Older children can appreciate the story of *The Young Landlords* (Myers, 1989), a group of boys who collaborate to buy and restore a dilapidated apartment building in their neighborhood. Examples of harmonious living span cultures and geographic regions. For example, *Crossing Bok Chitto: A Choctaw Tale of Friendship and Freedom* (Tingle, 2006) is a tale of friendship between Choctaw girl and enslaved African boy that illustrates responsibility to others' well-being.

In *Ogbo: Sharing Life in an African Village* (1996), Ifeoma Onyefulu shares her experiences growing up in an African village where age-defined peers interact as a kinship group, to contribute to the welfare of the larger community. Stories like these are fodder for discussion of impediments to and actions for supporting harmonious living.

H. B. Danesh (2006) acknowledges the challenges of harmonious living, but maintains that there is unity in diversity and diversity in unity. He defines unity as "the purposeful integration of two or more unique entities in a state of harmony and cooperation, resulting in the creation of a new evolving entity, usually of a higher order" (Danesh & Clarke-Habibi, 2007, p. 4) and maintains that diversity is an essential aspect of all life. The concept of unity in diversity establishes oneness, while diversity in unity "refers to the process of sharing different views, characteristics, needs and aspirations together as we pursue legitimate objectives within a united and just framework" (2007, p. 6).

Segregation is an obstacle to recognizing shared objectives because people who live and interact in homogeneous locales have limited opportunities to learn about attitudes, beliefs, experiences, and practices that are different from their own. In terms of understanding others, segregation, or the experience of "ethnic encapsulation" (Banks, 1997), may be most problematic for members of dominant cultures (Kruse, 2001).

Dominant culture refers to groups who are in the majority and/or have access to more power and resources than other groups, thus having dominant influence on values, language, and behavior (Giroux, 1989; Marshall, 1998). Members of dominant groups may experience little diversity in their own lives and see their own cultural experience overrepresented in the media, thus reinforcing an ethnocentric view of their own experience as "normal" and superior. While nondominant groups may be isolated in segregated living, they experience dominant culture, language, and ideology through media representations and school curriculum (Darder, 2012 Nieto, 2000).

In either case, scarcity of opportunities to interact with and come to know others with different perspectives perpetuates narrow thinking and inhibits the development of reciprocal relationships necessary for living in harmony.

Role of Youth Literature

Youth literature can cross the boundaries of personal experience and separation to allow children to learn about lived realities that vary from their own experiences (Kruse, 2001). Appreciating difference is vital, but it is equally important to recognize how unique traits and contributions *combine and blend together to create something powerful and beautiful* (Goldstein, 2004, p. 134). Youth literature provides occasions to recognize positive attributes and contributions of characters that represent people across the spectrum of diverse backgrounds and abilities. Interdependence, common goals, and examples of life lived harmoniously can be revealed through literature.

We Had a Picnic This Sunday Past (Woodson, 1997) is a story that presents a universal experience of family gatherings to share food and fellowship. The story depicts the unique individuals, dialogue, and traditions of her African American family. While the picnic takes place in a particular cultural context, the themes of family and fellowship are universal.

Maria's experiences in *Journey of the Sparrows* (Buss, 1997), as a refugee who flees to the United States after her family is killed by the government of El Salvador is, thankfully, less universal. Still, as readers become aware of the horrific circumstances, they can relate to her loss of family and home. Maria joins a community of refugees who work together, with love and compassion, to build new lives.

These examples present contrasting life circumstances, one of safety and stability and one of terror and uncertainty. Both, however, provide examples of ways that people can help each other to make life better.

Conflict Prevention

Respect for difference is a foundation for preventing conflict. Stereotypes negatively impact perceptions and beliefs about others, while bias negatively influences interactions and can lead to conflict. Even with positive intentions, differing perceptions of language, values, needs, and behaviors can create misunderstandings and perceptions of conflict. However, conflict can be minimized or transformed by countering stereotypes with understanding and acknowledging that discrimination and injustice have impacted the lives and opportunities of certain groups.

Terrible Things: An Allegory of the Holocaust (Bunting, 1999) uses bunnies as characters to introduce children to the concept of bias and understanding that good people are hurt by actions that stem from bias. The story also encourages readers to consider the importance of standing up for the rights of others.

Culturally conscious literature promotes understanding of real people within authentic contexts that help children understand how diversity can be framed in ways that stimulate and legitimize violence against others. For example, *As Long as the Rivers Flow: A Last Summer Before Residential School* (Loyie, 2008) and *Sweetgrass Basket* (Carvell, 2005) tell of Native American children who were forcibly removed from their families and placed in boarding schools designed to destroy their identities and cultures (Churchill, 2004; Pratt, 1890). The story conveys the rich environment of the home and tragic losses that children, families, and communities suffered from violent government policies.

Along with the aspects of diversity noted in the introduction to this chapter, understanding differences among and across groups becomes even more complex when we consider the contributions of anthropologist E. T. Hall (1969) who noted that perceptions of time, space organization, power, and relationships to nature differ among groups of people relative to social and physical contexts. Hall argues that these differences often lead to misunderstandings and miscommunication when individuals or groups assume that others share their own perceptions of reality. Failure to recognize the knowledge and culture of others can lead to stereotypes and perceptions that those who are different are deficient or dangerous (Derman-Sparks, 2010; Lantieri & Patti, 1996).

Conflict occurs naturally as part of the learning process in groups with different experiences, values, and beliefs (Nieto, 2006, p. 26). Sharing conflicting ideas can to lead to positive outcomes when students are guided to express themselves, hear other points of view and work toward mutual understanding. Respectful dialogue can lead to improved understandings and appreciation for multiple perspectives. In other words, conflicts that stem from cultural and racial bias can be a catalyst for teaching understanding of others and conflict transformation skills (Lantieri & Patti, 1996).

The human experience is complex and diverse; true understanding is only possible when all voices and experiences are embraced recognized as valid and valued (Darder, 2012). Those experiences include oppression and violence that is due to biases and stereotypes that privilege some while demeaning and dehumanizing others (Ashley, 2008).

Understanding conflict related to diversity is contingent upon understanding the ways that oppression of certain groups shaped history and impacts contemporary relationships. Discussions of story dynamics are a safe emotional space to consider the source of problems and possible solutions.

Role of Youth Literature

Mutually beneficial interactions depend upon perspectives and skills that are difficult to learn in the heat of personal conflict that challenges beliefs about identity and social relationships. Literary discussions provide opportunities to consider multiple perspectives and confront difficult issues with discussions of stories in emotional environments that are relatively safe.

With support from adults, children can learn to express and hear differing points of view as they grapple with the difficult issues that are encountered in authentic stories. Discussions can also foster empathy and support collaborative solutions to difficult problems.

All of a Kind Family (Taylor, 2011), *Papa Jethro* (Cohen, 2007), *Don't Sneeze at the Wedding* (Mayer, 2013) and *Always an Olivia: A Remarkable Family History* (Herron, 2012) are children's books that portray Jewish life and culture with universally appealing themes. The connections that youth make to characters in books like these promote empathy and prepare youth to recognize anti-Semitic rhetoric as biased and unjust.

Books about children's experiences can also reveal the suffering caused when bias and discrimination lead to hate and violence. *Benno and the Night of the Broken Glass* (Wiviott, 2014) and *The Devil in Vienna* (Orgel, 2004) portray the terror, agony, and destruction of lives that was inflicted on Jewish people during the Holocaust. *The Whispering Town* (Elvgren, 2014) and *Hidden: A Child's Story of the Holocaust* (Dauvillier, 2014) are stories of people who recognized injustice and took great risks to protect Jewish children from the Nazis. Stories of people who stood up for the rights of others can inspire and empower children to do the same. *Remember Not to Forget* (Finkelstein, 1993) is a picture book that documents anti-Semitism with photographs and text to demonstrate how biases and stereotypes shaped negative perceptions of Jewish people to the extent that the horrors of the Holocaust were accepted by large numbers of people.

Literature can offer insights that promote appreciation of individuals and different groups It can also help youth recognize the relationships between bias and perceptions, biased perceptions and the potential for conflict, and the destructive consequences of violence. Guided discussions can support critical thinking and prepare children to counter bias in ways that promote human dignity and equity for all.

Avoidance and Repair of Harm

Children's literature that features accurate portrayals of diverse groups and social issues promote understandings that are needed to avoid actions that cause harm to others (Reese, 2007; Yokota, 1993). Respect for difference and recognition of bias make it possible to identify sources of harm and develop strategies for reparation. Good stories can foster empathy and care as a foundation for caring about the welfare of others and the motivation for positive actions.

Each Kindness (Woodson, 2012), for example, tells the story of a young girl who repeatedly rejects offers of friendship from Maya because she is different, because she is poor. The protagonist realizes that she has hurt Maya when her teacher offers a lesson about kindness. She cannot make amends because Maya's family has moved on. The reader is left with the impression that the protagonist has become aware of the needs of others and intends to be more compassionate in future relationships. This book can be fodder for rich discussions about needs, difference, prejudice, as well as, the causes and implications of poverty. Along with developing sensitivity to the feelings and needs of others, the book encourages readers to reflect on ways that their own actions can help or hurt others.

Providing inclusive literature is an approach to teaching that avoids harm by ensuring that all children see themselves represented. Literature that truthfully depicts student's own experiences and cultures reinforces that they are equally valued and worthy. Opportunities to grapple with issues, questions, and problems that are relevant make learning meaningful and engaging. Literary experiences that embrace the lives of children support conditions for successful learning, while exclusion puts underrepresented children at a disadvantage.

Children's literature can mirror the reader's life or a window into the lives of others. By presenting characters with a range of abilities, religions, cultures, and abilities stories help children understand different ways of experiencing and representing the world (Mendoza & Reese, 2001). Acting in ways that avoid harm calls for abilities to interpret feelings and significant events in the lives of others. Culturally conscious social skills can be supported by using the experiences of characters in story to interpret events, empathize with feelings, and develop approaches to situations that are mutually respectful (Verden, 2012).

The potential to enhance, rather than diminish understanding, depends to a large extent on the sensitivity and authenticity of the literature (Colby & Lyon, 2004; Morgan, 2009; Sinclair, 2004). Accurate, high-quality literature affirms children from the represented groups and increases mutual understanding and respect across groups (Pires, 2011). Authentic literature portrays realities of human relationships and cultural significance through portrayals of characters in realistic settings (Seale & Dow, 2012). Inaccurate portrayals, however, demean the group being represented and promote faulty perceptions and stereotypical thinking about others (Mendoza & Reese, 2001).

Role of Youth Literature

Books about diversity address the universal themes of the human experience to which all readers can relate. Within universal themes, authentic literature places characters in settings and situations that accurately portray the cultures, knowledge, perspectives, and lived experiences of particular groups of people. The following examples address literature and Native American cultures, however, the principles of authentic representations in literature apply to any group of people. Native American authors who write with an insider's perspective lend authenticity to high-quality literature that affirms identity, informs others, and reflects the realities of a diverse world (Reese, 2007). *The People Shall Continue* (Ortiz, 1988) is a history of interactions between Native American peoples and European settlers that includes violent and oppressive events but emphasizes that all people can contribute to the good of all. *When the Shadbush Blooms* (Messinger, 2007) is narrated by a Lenni Lenape girl whose portrayals of family life during a time of pre-European contact are contrasted with corresponding photos of a contemporary Lenni Lenape family. A great-great-grandmother tells her family about the efforts of the Ojibway people to maintain their way of life in *Night Flying Woman: An Ojibway Narrative* (Broker, 1983). *Hidden Roots* tells the story of an Abenaki family to reveal the impact of the Vermont Eugenics Project that targeted Native Americans for force sterilization (Bruchac, 2004). *Shi-shi-etko* (Campbell, 2008) narrates the experiences of Native children who were forced to leave loving families and attend boarding schools far from home. *who will tell my brother?* (Carvell, 2004) grapples with ongoing cultural oppression as Evan attempts to change his school's use of a Native image for its mascot. Contemporary life and Native American culture is portrayed in *Jingle Dancer* (Smith, 2000) through a picture book telling of a suburban girl who prepares for her first jingle dance at a powwow. For older youth, *Indian Shoes* (Smith, 2002) and *The Absolutely True Diary of a Part-time Indian* (Alexie, 2007) portray contemporary culture in stories of growing up that connect with any reader.

Youth literature that depicts authentic lives can increase understanding across the boundaries of cultural differences.

Conversely, inauthentic literature furthers the divide by fostering misconceptions and demeaning individuals and groups.

Arrow to the Sun (McDermott, 1997) is a Caldecott Award winner and widely used by educators in spite of numerous inaccuracies in the portrayal of Pueblo people and culture (Reese, 2006). The book presents Pueblo culture as sort of generic rather than noting that many distinct Pueblos have unique cultures and beliefs. The kiva in *Arrow to the Sun*, for example, is depicted as an ominous place of trial rather than a community gathering place of instruction and ceremonies. The insensitive and inaccurate portrayal of the kiva misrepresents and trivializes cherishes aspects of Pueblo culture and life while misinforming readers outside the community. According to Reese, these errors are problematic for both insiders and outsiders. When used in a classroom setting, Pueblo children are conflicted between knowing that the book is wrong and their respect for the teacher. The resulting tension impairs the children's abilities to engage in meaningful learning (Reese, 2006). The inaccurate presentation promotes misconceptions that prevent understanding of Pueblo culture by children outside community.

Teaching about diversity is a vital aspect of teaching for peace and literature is an effective resource when used with care. Because diversity is so wide-ranging, it is important for adults to commit to continuous learning. No one can be an expert on every aspect of diversity, but background research can be done to best ensure that the literature communicates accurate information.

Social Justice

A peace-oriented curriculum includes social justice by addressing discrimination and exploitation, recognizing the contributions of nondominant groups and identifying aspects of social violence. Equally important, it promotes awareness of the peaceful movements for change from which society benefits.

Literature is a powerful means of confronting difficult and painful issues related to oppression and privilege by portraying the lives of compelling characters in authentic settings. Realistic stories can portray the strengths and contributions of all people and clarify the role that bias and discrimination has historically played in rendering certain groups vulnerable to injustice and deprivation. For example, the internment of a Japanese American family during World War II is the setting for *Baseball Saved US* (Mochizuki, 1995), while *Freedom on the Menu: The Greensboro Sit-ins* (Weatherford, 2007) tells the story of peaceful demonstrations against racial discrimination.

Literature can also promote awareness of current conditions such as child labor, exploitive labor practices, and slavery. *Working Cotton* (Williams, 1997) illustrates conditions that children and families face as migrants who work for low wages. A more comprehensive view of working children is found in *Listen to Us: The World's Working Children* (Springer, 1997).

Children can also learn about peaceful actions to achieve positive change. *Dolores Huerta* (Warren, 2012) was a teacher, who became an activist for farm worker rights when she learned about the struggles of her student's families that were caused by subsistence wages and exploitive labor practices. *We've Got a Job: The 1963 Children's March* (Levinson, 2012) shows children who risked jail to protest injustice and segregation in pursuit of equal rights. These stories can inspire as they demonstrate that positive change is possible.

Guided discussions about the issues portrayed in literature allow youth to construct understandings. They are able to critically consider social dynamics that contribute to inequities by considering the multiple perspectives presented in authentic texts. With support from caring adults they may respond in ways that promote justice and well-being for all.

While teaching young people to understand and value diversity is vital, teaching for peace is not cultural relativism or passive acceptance of oppressive practices (Brandt, 1994). On the contrary, the very beliefs and actions that violate human rights undermine peace. Rather than avoiding uncomfortable topics, diversity education in pursuit of peace, confronts injustice, promotes human rights and responsibilities, equality and justice for all (Brandt, 1994; Goldstein, 2004).

Oppression and privilege are often unrecognized due to societal emphases on personal responsibility and individual achievement that fail to take into account historical examples of discrimination and exploitation (Adams, Bell, & Griffin, 2007). The dominant narrative does not fully address the experiences of individuals and groups who were historically denied acknowledgement and rewards for significant contributions because of biases and discriminatory laws and policies (Banks, 2003; Nieto, 2006). Denying or ignoring history masks conditions that oppress certain groups and perpetuates the myth of equal opportunity (Bynoe, 2004).

Social justice issues are often difficult to teach because they are, by nature, uncomfortable. Understanding the dynamics of injustice requires that certain groups recognize their own privilege (Freire, 1990; Kendall, 2012). Failure to address social injustice, however, silences groups and perpetuates prejudice (Ching, 2005; Darder, 2012; Pires, 2011), while addressing it promotes cultural sensitivity and mutual understanding that are necessary for positive intergroup relationships (Tharp, 2012).

Role of Youth Literature

Inclusive literature offers a venue for critical inquiry into the human experience and ways that social dynamics frame lives. Children can recognize aspects of social privilege and oppression through authentic depictions of lives lived in various circumstances (Steiner, 2008). When encountering characters about which they care, youth are able to reconsider biased perceptions of others and consider the social conditions that cause inequities and suffering.

Awareness and recognition of injustice is not enough. Without hope and possibilities for action to achieve change, youth may be left with only anger and depression. Fortunately, youth literature offers examples of peaceful responses to injustice that have made positive differences.

That's Not Fair!: Emma Tenayuca's Struggle for Justice/ No Es Justo!: La lucha de Emma Tenayuca por la justicia (Tafolla & Yeneyuca, 2008) is based on the true story of young Emma's encounters with hungry children and desperately poor families that made her aware of injustice within her community. With her grandfather's help she learns that some groups of people are not paid fairly and struggle to survive, while other people from other groups have much more than they need. With small acts of kindness, she helps those in need. As a woman, Emma organizes and strikes that result in higher wages. This story gives insight into causes of poverty and inspiration for action. The breadth of Emma's lifetime advocating for workers illustrates that change is possible with commitment and perseverance.

Questions to Consider for Diversity through Youth Literature

From Evaluation Criteria for Youth Literature in Peace Education

Copyright Candice C. Carter and Shelly Clay-Robison

1. Does the story positively portray (ethnic, racial, gender, sexual identity, cultural, ability, etc.) differences?
2. Are readers encouraged to see themselves as part of the larger society?
3. Are readers encouraged to empathize with members of other groups?
4. Is there respect and appreciation for other ways of living?
5. Does the author have an in-depth view of the cultural groups illustrated or is the author an "outsider" looking in?
6. Is the story culturally accurate?

7. Is there richness in detail to describe cultural groups or are cultural stereotypes reinforced?
8. Are "minority" groups added with a purpose?
9. Is the setting illustrated with authenticity and with detail?
10. Does it have a range of family roles?
11. Are there images of groups of people or individuals from different backgrounds interacting positively with each other?
12. Are diverse characters portrayed as empowered, or does the literature feature structural conflict in society?

Summary

Youth literature can make important contributions to helping youth develop orientations toward peaceful interactions between and among diverse groups of people. Universal themes, with diverse characters and contexts, allow readers to relate to people who are, in some ways, different from themselves. Authentic literature counters stereotypes, challenges biased notions, and promotes mutual respect and understanding. Telling the stories of underrepresented groups supports appreciation for diversity along with awareness of social inequity. Social issues become apparent within a context where readers are able to empathize with characters and become aware of sources of conflict and conditions of injustice. Using inclusive literature can foster dispositions, perceptions, and actions that support human dignity, justice, and equity.

4

Language Usage

Francisco Gomes de Matos (2008) describes language as "a mental marvel used for meaning-making" (p.1) and notes that effective communication is a primary focus of education, although there is scant attention to learning methods of peaceful communication. Thinking and language can be powerful means of promoting well-being and connections with others, but too often education serves to shape thinking in moralistic terms without compassionate connections (Rosenberg, 2003a). This chapter focuses on the need to learn "the language of life" (Rosenberg, 2005b, p. 24). Literature can help people understand the power of language in relation to achieving the conditions necessary for peace.

Construal of Peace

Literature has long been used to socialize and teach children moral lessons (Armstrong, 2003; Steiner, 2008). Themes and characters are obvious elements for shaping the message, but the language of the story carries powerful and often unexamined ideas. Literature is language and offers opportunities to explore, understand, and practice peaceful orientations (Morgan, 2009).

Children from around the world share ideas about peace in *What Does Peace Feel Like?* Radunsky (2004) uses the language of children to begin exploring the meaning of peace and to help them make connections to their own lives. *Peace Begins with You* (Scholes, 1990) is a comprehensive introduction to broader concepts about peace. It discusses aspects of living, including meeting needs, caring for others, and solving problems without violence. The discussion provides language that children need to form concepts, understand the dynamics of living together, and to consider the consequences of violence. The book encourages children to promote positive change by learning about themselves and others, becoming involved in decisions, considering different perspectives, and speaking up when something is wrong to promote positive change.

In addition to helping children learn to use a language of peace, literature can help them transform communication by recognizing, critiquing, and reframing language that demeans others or promotes violence (Ashley, 2008; Oxford, 2013). Through literature, children and adults can work together to critically consider the text and develop knowledge of the impact that language and dialogic practices have on relationships and interactions (Wong, 2009).

A language of peace is, foremost, grounded in the belief that peace is both desirable and possible through empathy and respect for others and commitment to the well-being of all (Gomes de Matos, 2008; Oxford, 2013, Rosenberg, 2003). Rebecca Oxford offers a general definition of the language of peace as "any form of communication—verbal or nonverbal—that describes, reflects, expresses, or actively expands peace" (2013, p. 1).

Language plays an important role in shaping the beliefs, perceptions, and dispositions that make peace work possible (Ashley, 2008). To believe that peace is desirable, or even possible, depends to a large extent on perceptions about the character and the worth of others. Those perceptions and resulting abilities to make caring connections are swayed by exposure to language that affirms or demeans differences (Gay, 1999; Gomes de Matos, 2008). Referring to individuals and groups in positive ways promotes respect for the inherent dignity and worth of all people. Mutual respect lays a foundation for the positive interactions and dialogue needed to live and work in harmony.

Using a language of peace can prevent or transform conflict when it stems from caring relationships and a desire for understanding. Marshall Rosenberg (2005) describes nonviolent communication as a means for developing mutual understanding and arriving at solutions that take the needs, interests, and values of all into account. Peaceful problem solving involves learning how to make empathetic connections, use respectful vocabulary, and engage in solution-oriented dialogue.

Role of Youth Literature

Literature can help youth to make empathetic connections to others through vicariously experiencing stories that reveal a character's needs and feelings. Discussions help youth develop a vocabulary to identify and understand their own feelings and needs while developing the ability to listen empathetically to others. *Peace a Vision for a New Generation* (Carter, 1993) was written by former President Jimmy Carter to address the need for young people to learn how to problem solving through "compromise and negotiation before they erupt into violence" (p. 198). He addresses comprehensive causes of conflict along with skills and methods to promote peace.

Stories that depict a range of realistic characters, experiences, and contexts allow readers to view others as complete people. Realistic perceptions of others make it possible to think critically about how language can affirm or demean groups of people. *A Gift from Papa* (Saenz, 1998), for example, is a bilingual story that depicts unique cultural aspects of a Mexican American family in the context of a story that has universal relevance and appeal. The story counters stereotypes and fosters respect for the characters who portray family life.

We Can Get Along: A Child's Book of Choices (Payne, 1997) depicts personal interactions and problems that are familiar to children along with various options for behaviors. Reading and discussing the book provides opportunities for children to think critically and creatively about the consequences of different actions. *Peace Week in Miss Foxe's Class* (Spinelli, 2009) shows children developing ideas and guidelines when their teacher declares that there will be no fighting for an entire week. The book helps children make connections between feelings and behaviors and illustrates strategies for coping with problems.

Harmonious Living

The *MacMillan Dictionary* (2014) defines *harmony* as "a situation in which people live and work well with other people, or in a way that does not damage things around them." *The Illustrated Oxford American Dictionary* (DK, 2003) defines it as an agreement or concord and lists synonyms that include "amicability, fellowship, cooperation, unity, oneness, concert and rapport."

Literature can help children understand ways that people work together to promote goodwill and reduce conflict. Stories offer opportunities to examine the role of language in shaping relationships and to encourage the goodwill needed for cooperative living. Realistic portrayals of characters affirm the whole person and promote positive perceptions of people from diverse backgrounds.

Interactions between characters in stories provide vicarious experiences that allow reflection upon emotional responses language and the resulting impact on social dynamics. *Chicora and the Little People: The Legend of Indian Corn, A Lumbee Tale* (Boughman, 2010) demonstrates how children are valued in indigenous societies and conveys the message that everyone has wisdom and contributes to society (Garcia, 2014). The story uses interactions between children and adults to demonstrate the benefits of listening and honoring the contributions of all.

Through literature, youth can experience and identify language that promotes respect, as well as demeaning language that causes division. Children relate to the narrative experiences and gain insights into how identity and perceptions of others are influenced by language.

Amicable living can be difficult even among groups bound together by love and commitment. Language that promotes respect and understanding shapes goodwill that is necessary for caring about others, working through problems, and finding ways to cooperate. Human beings are predisposed toward compassion and helping others, but socialization systems based on judgmental thinking undermine respect and stifle abilities to collaborate for meeting common needs (Rosenberg, 2003b). Peaceful language and communication skills can transform that divisive orientation to develop caring relationships aimed at "making life more wonderful" for everyone (Rosenberg, 2005b, p. 24).

Language that affirms the dignity and worth of others fosters empathy and respect for those who serve as a foundation seeking mutual understanding and acceptance of differences (Gay, 1999; Gomes de Matos, 2008). That foundation is necessary to develop harmonious relationships and take collective action that considers varying interests and values to find solutions that meet the needs of all (Oxford, 2013).

Role of Youth Literature

Narrative, which depicts the human experience and affirms difference, allows youth to develop respectful perceptions and recognition that diverse others can contribute to the good of all. Literature that depicts examples of language in the context of harmonious interactions offers opportunities for learning how to hear and communicate needs and find solutions in peaceful ways.

Waterlily, for example, illustrates the interdependent and cooperative nature of Dakota life during the nineteenth century (Deloria, 1990). To be Dakota was:

> to keep the rules imposed by kinship for achieving civility, good manners and a sense of responsibility to every individual dealt with. Thus only was it possible to live communally with success; that is to say, with a minimum of friction and a maximum of good will. (p. x)

The Dakota approach to teaching children desired behavior was consistent with expectations. Adults conveyed that honor and joy come from contributing to the welfare of others and children learned cooperative behaviors through modeling and gentle guidance. The following passage illustrates the power of compassionate language to guide shape perspective and guide behavior according to cultural values:

> Obviously he had been carefully trained, as only painstaking grandparents could train a child—with careful suasion. "That is not done, grandchild," they said quietly, or "Nobody does that," meaning "and neither ought you." No cross words, no whipping, just those simple words of correction, in kindly tones, were remarkably effective. The very calmness of grandparents soothed a child and made him inclined to obey. (p. 24)

This example of disposition and the language used to guide the behavior of children in traditional Dakota culture embodies aspects of peaceful communication. The grandparents' gentle demeanor conveyed respect while guiding the child toward behaviors that aligned with the values of the community. Discussions could lead to reflection of student's own experiences to examination and critique underlying beliefs and values related to cooperation versus force and an examination of the consequences of the different approaches.

Conflict Prevention

Language plays an important role in creating perceptions of others as potential partners or as adversaries who cannot be trusted. Affirmations of diversity allow for appreciating different beliefs, values, and knowledge, as well as, skills and abilities that contribute to the well-being of all (Gay, 1999; Oxford, 2013). Conversely, language can encourage negative views of others by demeaning differences and fostering perceptions that some groups are superior to others (Rosenberg, 2005b). Conflicts arise when those views are used to justify inequities in access to resources and inequality of status and participation in society.

Literature allows children to observe interactions between characters, relate to feelings and identify how language impacts behavior. *The Crocodile and the Ghost Bat Have a Hullabaloo* (Sapp, 2006) begins with the animals of the forest agreeing to gather for a shared meal and fellowship. The event begins with cooperation and consideration for others; some animals prefer nighttime and some prefer daytime, so they compromise by meeting at twilight. Everyone enjoys the time together, until Crocodile and Ghost Bat have a misunderstanding. Ghost Bat insults Crocodile with "At least I don't let my food rot before I eat it." Crocodile was most offended because the taunt was based on a stereotype that she had worked hard to dispel. Soon, other animals join the conflict by calling each other names and their celebration is destroyed. The story offers opportunities to examine cooperation in addition to the harm caused by stereotypes and harmful language, as well as to explore strategies for resolving the conflict.

The ability to transform conflict into opportunities for positive change depends to a significant degree on how participants perceive of each other, and those perceptions are influenced by language. Creating conditions of understanding, respect, and equity that are needed to avoid or transform conflict also means recognizing and eliminating language that judges, demeans, and divides.

Everyone has needs and at times, those needs appear to conflict with the needs of others. While conflict is natural and can lead to positive outcomes, conflict can also have painful consequences. Marshal Rosenberg (2003a) maintains that thinking and speaking in terms of moralistic judgments blocks understanding of feelings and needs that are at the root of the conflict. Expressing needs and listening empathetically to the needs of others fosters compassionate connections that are necessary for cooperatively seeking solutions. Thinking and speaking in terms that acknowledge the needs underlying actions contribute to understandings that can transform conflict and promote unity. Peaceful communications rely on viewing conflicts constructively, addressing others with respect and empathy, avoiding harmful language and perceiving others as peace partners (Gomes de Matos, 2008).

Language shapes perceptions that influence how we think of others and ourselves; hence it plays an important role in determining the tone of inte ractions and outcome of conflicts (Ashley, 1999; Hall 1976; Rosenberg, 2003a). Positive perceptions of individuals and groups as potential partners allow for constructive approaches to conflict. Likewise, viewing others with respect supports dialogue that promotes cooperation rather than coercion.

Violent language undermines the empathy, mutual understanding, and respect that are necessary for peaceful interactions. Racist, sexist, classist, and xenophobic language hurt and demean members of the group to which the terms are addressed. They also create "enemy images" that portray people as wrong, bad, or deficient, causing division and distrust (Rosenberg, 2005b). Stereotypes define members of groups in terms of moralistic judgments rather as people who have common needs and feelings. When groups are deemed "gangs, or terrorists" they are marked as enemies, not human beings with whom it might be possible to find common ground and make peace (Ashley, 2008). Those perceptions influence communication and diminish respectful dialogue.

Role of Youth Literature

Unbiased views of others lay the foundation for constructive responses to conflict. Literature can, first, realistically portray different groups to develop respectful language and perceptions of others (Mendoza & Reese, 2001). Well-developed characters provide insights into feelings, needs, and behaviors across virtually all groups of people and a multitude of conflict situations (Steiner, 2008). Youth are able to connect with characters and relate to the needs and feelings of others in diverse contexts; those experiences can inform interactions with people in their own lives.

Literature also provides opportunities to explore how conflict is created through bias and stereotypes with examples of how language shapes beliefs about others and motivates actions that are based on those beliefs. A classic novel for teens, *The Outsiders* (Hinton, 2006), addresses issues of bias and privilege that lead to tragic consequences. The story revolves around conflict between two groups of teenagers, the low-income "Greasers" and the well-to-do "Socs." They are separated and defined by social class and perceive each other through stereotypes as enemies. Those beliefs lead to physical conflicts that result in deaths on both sides. Hinton's characters are portrayed as full human beings with feelings and needs that could be common ground for mutual understanding and respect. The scenes and dialogue in this novel offer multiple opportunities for youth to deconstruct language that fosters biased thinking, negative emotions, and violent actions. At the same time, individual characters elicit empathy and convey feelings and needs on both sides of the conflict. Connections to the characters make it possible for youth to analyze how language contributed to the problem and consider how it could have been used differently to foster respect and nonviolent interactions.

Avoidance and Repair of Harm

Clearly, the elimination of overtly violent language is a critical step toward avoiding harm. Insults are intended to degrade and hurt individuals; racist, sexist, classist, and xenophobic language is used to communicate inferiority of certain groups. Literature is a means for youth to confront hurtful language, empathize with characters, and grapple with the implications and consequences of its use. Reflections and discussions around the effects of violent language can prepare youth to respond in ways that transform language and promote peace.

Even among well-intended people, harm can be caused inadvertently through misconceptions and communication that is perceived differently by participants. Regional and cultural differences in vocabulary and discourse style can be interpreted differently to create negative perceptions. Literature can expose youth to varying communication styles and ways of perceiving information to foster sensitivity to difference and approaches to clarifying meaning.

Terms within a lexicon represent perspectives. In particular, terms that refer to groups of people represent a range of perspectives about differences in ethnicity, race, gender, religion, and other groups. Whether the terms are negative, neutral, or positive, they communicate values that give structure to consciousness (Ashley, 1999). Continued exposure to words that carry negative connotations diminish self-esteem and foster bias against others.

Edward T. Hall was a pioneer of intercultural communication who spent decades studying different cultures and identified elements of communication that often lead to misunderstandings and potentially to hostility. Hall (1969, 1976) emphasized that communication encompasses more than words and that even words can be ambiguous. Meaning is contextually bound and influenced by perceptions of time, space, body language, power, and unspoken expectations.

Combined with the elements of nonverbal communication outlined by Hall, the relative meaning of words themselves makes mutual understanding a challenge (Ashley, 1999). Fortunately, learning about others and the many influences on communication can help to avoid unintentional harm and foster mutual understanding. In addition, learning to use dialogic practices that clarify meaning make it possible to repair harm by addressing misunderstandings.

Role of Youth Literature

Same Sun Here (House & Vaswani, 2011) is the story of two children who meet when they sign up for a school pen pal project. Through letters, Meena, a 12-year-old girl who has immigrated to New York from India, becomes close friends with River, a 12-year-od boy who lives in the mountains of Kentucky with his grandmother. Their story is told through a series of letters that show the development of a personal relationship and address many social issues. Because of the diverse backgrounds of the characters, the dialogue within the letters shows both how easily misunderstandings can occur and how a foundation of caring and respect can allow for clarification and deeper understanding.

It is important to note that the children had agreed to be honest and that they could tell each other anything. As the children share daily experiences along with thoughts regarding serious issues, potential conflicts arose within their cherished friendship. In an exchange of letters, Meena tells of being called a terrorist by a stranger. River empathized with the pain Meena felt, but explained that at one time he once might have thought the same thing because he had never been exposed to people who were different. He explains that he doesn't want to hurt her, but needs to tell the truth. At this point, they have established a foundation of care and are able to voice uncomfortable truths with language that communicates compassion. Sharing those truths furthers their understanding and trust.

In another example, River tells Meena that he has an Indian physician, Dr. Patel, who is close to his family. He also comments on the doctor's "funny" accent and that his grandmother had reprimanded him for staring at Mrs. Patel's bindi. Meena responded by telling him that she also had an accent and that it hurts to be laughed at. She emphasizes the depth of the pain by saying she couldn't be a friend to someone who laughed at her way of speaking. She tells him about the bindi and explains how uncomfortable she feels when people stare at her because she is different. River apologizes, explaining that he didn't mean to be rude, but that he was interested in the difference. He further explained that he understood about people making fun of different ways of talking and that the accent of his region was often the butt of jokes.

The exchanges between Meena and River illustrate how easily harm can be caused without malicious intent, but out of ignorance. It also shows how responses that are clear about the harm caused, but without judgment of the person, can clarify needs, misunderstandings, and in this case, strengthen relationships. Discussion of the meanings and misunderstanding in the story can create a forum for youth to make connections to their own lives. Sharing experiences when they misunderstood someone or were misunderstood allow for exploring perceptions and developing strategies for promoting mutual understanding.

Fulfillment of Needs

The ability of all people to meet basic needs is a foundation for peaceful living that requires concern for others and understanding of interdependence in order to fulfill one's own needs in consideration for the needs of others. Basic needs have been identified in different ways and to varying degrees of specificity. Human needs include physical needs for safety, security, and sustenance along with emotional and psychological needs for identity, belonging and participation, leisure and play, spirituality and love, integrity and autonomy (Costanza et al., 2007; Deci & Ryan, 2000; Maslow, 1943; Rosenberg, 2003a).

While all people share the same basic needs, access and approaches to meeting those needs differ. Literature provides a lens to recognize common needs and insights into diverse approaches to living. Equally important, literature can reveal social dynamics that create inequity, perceptions of conflicting needs, and demonstrate cooperative living to ensure the well-being of all.

Nonviolent communication (NVC) stems from a belief that all action serves as an attempt to meet needs (Rosenberg, 2003a, 2003b, 2005a, 2005b). Depending on awareness and disposition, the consequences of those actions have the potential to benefit others through cooperation or to create conflict by denying the needs of other people. According to Rosenberg, attempts to meet needs through coercion or force, ultimately, have negative consequences, but cooperative approaches are mutually beneficial. NVC provides guidance for developing communication skills that allow understanding and compassionate connections that allow people to give and receive "out of the joy that springs forth whenever we willingly enrich another person's life" (2003a, p. 5).

Communicating needs through NVC begins with approaching interactions with awareness of feelings and identifying the conditions that create them. For example feelings like hope, joy, and confidence indicate that needs are met, while anger, fear, and sadness are clues to discovering what need is unmet. Unfortunately, feelings are often not recognized in relation to needs but instead projected onto the behaviors of others. Certain behaviors may well trigger feelings, but the feeling is the clue that leads to identifying the unmet need and seeking assistance from another to behave in a way that will allow that need to be met.

Clearly expressing feelings and needs makes it possible for others to connect empathetically and motivates cooperation by drawing upon the inherent pleasure that comes from helping others. Requests for help in the form of clearly articulated, concrete actions allow people to negotiate and make mutually beneficial solutions possible. Along with expressing needs, the process involves observing and listening to understand the feelings and needs of others.

Role of Youth Literature

A variety of children's books are available that can be used to help children understand feelings and to teach words and strategies regulating behavior and communicating needs. Simple picture books can help older children, as well as very young children, make connections between feelings, needs, and ways to express them (Brindley & Laframboise, 2001). Mercer Mayer has written many books that deal with everyday situations, relationships, and feelings that are common to young children. *I Was So Mad* (Mayer, 1983) takes the reader through a series of situations in which an adult thwarts Little Critter's endeavors. To each situation he responds, "I was so mad." The story is an enjoyable read but on the surface offers little in terms helping children learn to use language for meeting needs.

It does, however, offer multiple opportunities to explore the feelings that Little Critter experienced, identify possible needs that prompted his actions, and explore ways that Little Critter's needs could be met that would be agreeable to the adults in his life. For example, when he paints pictures on the house and Grandpa stops him, Little Critter becomes angry. On the surface, he is angry because Grandpa won't let him paint on the house, but it is worth exploring the need that prompted Little Critter to paint on the house. Perhaps he was trying to be helpful or needed to express himself through pictures. Discussing Grandpa's needs might lead to identifying ways to meet the needs of both. Perhaps finding another place that Litter Critter could paint that would be amenable to both. Children will be able to make connections to their own experiences and feelings through guided discussion and with help, can develop language that they can use in similar situations.

Social and Legal Justice

"If we expect students to become stewards of social justice and proponents of cultural diversity, they need to be properly armed with the language to articulate the experiences and realities of their past, present and future." (Tharp, 2012). Literature offers a context for learning about multiple realities. Text and discussion help to develop understanding about concepts of social justice with language to frame and question beliefs and understandings about self and others and practices of oppression and privilege. When youth are able to recognize language that shapes perceptions that make violence and inequity seem normal and acceptable, they are better able to resist its influence and support equality.

The preamble to *The Universal Declaration of Human Rights* states, "Whereas recognition of the inherent dignity and of the equal and inalienable rights of all members of the human family is the foundation of freedom, justice and peace in the world..." (United Nations General Assembly, 1948). Yet, oppression and privilege continue, enabled by apathy and supported with laws and policies that, throughout history, have legitimized denial of human rights.

According to Ashley (2008), acceptance and perpetuation of violence against others requires two things; the first is "the dehumanization of the people toward whom the violence is or may be directed." Biased language and stereotypes create misconceptions and demean certain groups and can foster perceptions that they, rather than oppressive social conditions, are responsible for inequities. The second factor involves "renaming the actual acts of violence in functional ways" (p. 76). For example, the term "corporal punishment" is still a legal form of disciplining children in schools

(Morones, 2013). The benign sounding term encompasses acts that range from gentle swats to brutal beatings and electrical shock (Human Rights Watch, 2008).

Those two factors are essential to understanding how discriminatory practices and policies that sanction social violence can come to be considered not only acceptable but even just by whole groups of people. Literature can help youth understand the role that language plays in shaping social thought to sanction the direct, cultural, and structural violence that perpetuates inequality (Ashley, 1999, Madhuri, Han, & Laughter, 2012; Tharp, 2012).

A critical framework (Lewison, Flint, & Van Sluys, 2001) can be used to guide youth to name and examine social justice issues through literature and make connections to their own lives. Considering social justice in text allows readers to perceive daily life through new lenses and view the world through different perspectives, while recognizing the relationships between language and power for making changes in everyday life (Madhuri, Han & Laughter, 2013).

Picower (2012) suggests six categories for organizing studies of social justice issues: 1) developing self-love and knowledge, 2) developing respect for others, 3) exploring how diversity has impacted certain groups, 4) learning about social movements and social change, 5) raising awareness of issues, and 6) taking social action.

Role of Youth Literature

Positive self-concepts and respect for others lays a foundation for understanding social issues and concepts of human rights. *Mine & Yours: Human Rights for Kids* (Berry, 2005) and *For Every Child: The Rights of the Child in Words and Pictures* (Castle, 2002) introduce concepts and language for understanding and talking about social justice. *I Have the Right to Be a Child* (Serres, 2012) and *Stand Up for Your Rights* (Atgwa, Bakyayita, & Boltauzer, 2000) reinforce understanding of foundations for peaceful living. This literature calls attention to the ways that rights can be denied, and it introduces possibilities for peaceful avoidance of those situations. Encountering familiar situations in diverse contexts allows the reader to reconsider beliefs about what is normal and to become aware of other possibilities. When they engage with literature that presents positive language and portrayals of characters that are both similar and different to them, youth can reflect on unexamined aspects of their own lives in relation to others. The knowledge and language presented through literature can help youth develop ways of thinking about self and others as worthy and deserving of human rights.

Children's literature presents many opportunities for children to frame positive identities and positive perceptions of others. Nolan's *What I Like about Me!* (2009) and *The Okay Book* (Parr, 2011) are board books that introduce young children to a variety of ways to be different. The range of characteristics guarantees that most children will be able to relate something to their own experience. The recurring language "it's okay" serves as a basis for forming positive perceptions of self and appreciation for diversity. *What I Like about Me!* (Nolan, 2009) and *I Like Myself!* (Beaumont, 2010) reinforce positive perceptions about difference and understanding one's self. *Jacob's Dress* (Hoffman, 2014) and *William's Doll* (Zolotow, 1985) are positive portrayals of boys whose preferences challenge gender stereotypes.

Books can affirm children who have differing abilities and foster understanding of both the challenges and strengths that face everyone. *The Black Book of Colors* (Cottin, 2010) encourages readers to imagine the world without sight. The narrator in *I Have a Sister—My Sister is Deaf* (Peterson, 1984) celebrates a loving relationship with a sister who just happens to be deaf. Lola A. Schaefer (2008) helps children understand and appreciate others with health and ability differences. Through her *Understanding Differences* series, she helps children understand deafness and mobility. The knowledge presented in these books support language to talk and think about differing abilities that affirms the worth, dignity, and rights of all people.

Learning about daily life in diverse contexts creates a lens through which the ordinary becomes unusual and allows youth to think critically about their own lives and in relationship to the experiences of other people. *Somewhere in the World Right Now* (Schuett, 1997) helps youth see their own position within the larger world through depictions of people all over the world doing different things at any given time. Books that provide images of the diversity of the daily lives allow for understanding common needs and characteristics, as well as ways that the social contexts influence behaviors, beliefs, and approaches to life.

Authentic literature provides vocabulary to frame accurate perceptions of others and consider how privilege and oppression have impacted diverse groups of people differently. Books are available to allow youth to encounter a wide range of topics that represent diverse experiences and multiple perspectives. For example, in *Tasting the Sky: A Palestinian Childhood*, Barakat (2007) provides insights into the daily life in Palestine, and *If I Ever Get Out of Here* (Gansworth, 2013) is a teen's story of life on a Tuscarora reservation. *Pancho Rabbit and the Coyote: A Migrant's Tale* (Tonatiuh, 2013) portrays the challenges and joys of a family of newcomers to the United States. *Notes From a Melanin Son* (Woodson, 2010) addresses the challenges of growing up and explores issues facing biracial, blended, and LGBT families. Readers can experience the lived realities and emotional impact of poverty in *The Junction of Sunshine and Lucky* (Schindler, 2014). *When the Horses Ride by: Children in the Times of War* (Greenfield, 2006) gives insights into the effects of war.

Literature can also help youth understand the impact of structural oppression. Through stories told in *If the People Could Fly: American Black Folk Tales* (Hamilton, 1985), readers of all backgrounds can relate to the despair caused by the failure to recognize the human rights of all races of people and the inhumanity of slavery. They can also appreciate the strength and resilience of the people who survived. The Holocaust is another clear example of the tragic consequences of extreme bias against a particular group of people. Told through the harrowing experiences of a child, *The Boy in the Striped Pajamas* (Bynoe, 2008) allows readers to make personal connections to and recognize how biased thinking was used to implement laws and oppressive practices.

January's Sparrow (Polacco, 2009) tells the story of a slave family's escape to the free North where they continued to live in fear because of laws that allowed slave catchers to capture and reclaim them as property. The story clearly depicts the horrors of living as a slave, but instead of portraying the family only as victims, it illustrates their love, strength, and courage in the context of the most trying conditions. It also shows that even with inhuman laws in place, there were some people who were willing to stand up for what is right.

Many examples of youth literature portray individuals and groups who were committed to social justice. These examples give children language to name problems, to consider solutions, and to inspire their own actions. *Who Will Tell My Brother?* tells the story of a Native American teens efforts to change the offensive Native image that was used as his school's mascot. *Planting the Trees of Kenya: The Story of Wangari Maathai* (Nivoli, 2008) communicates the difference one woman could make by planting trees. *Delivering Justice: W. W. Law and the Fight for Civil Rights* (Haskins, 2006) and *Claudette Colvin: Twice Toward Justice* (Hoose, 2010) are examples of individual efforts contributed to the Civil Rights Movement.

Books about social movements illustrate the importance of communication for mutual understanding and power of groups who work together for positive change. *With Courage and Cloth: Winning the Fight for a Woman's Right to Vote* (Bausum, 2009) tells of the collective struggle to achieve full participation in society for women. The stories of courageous people who risked defying the law in Nazi Germany in order to do what was right are told in *Saving Children from the Holocaust: The Kindertransport* (Byers, 2012). Susan Terkel (1996) gives an overview of social movements and the potential to effect positive change in *People Power: A Look at Nonviolent Action and Defense*.

Questions to Consider for Language in Youth Literature

From Evaluation Criteria for Youth Literature in Peace Education

Copyright Candice C. Carter and Shelly Clay-Robison

1. Is language comprehensible to targeted audience?
2. Is the presentation engaging?
3. Does it stimulate the reader's affect?
4. Is the language too scary for the targeted audience?
5. Is the language gender/sex biased?
6. Does the use of language depict any characters as typically disempowered?
7. Does it use realistic dialogue between characters?
8. Does it promote understanding of nontransliteral concepts in different languages?
9. Does the text feature usage of nonviolent communication?

Summary

A language of peace encompasses more than words. Communication depends on understanding the context, including beliefs, values, and perceptions, that vary across individuals and groups. Peace also depends on recognizing language that escalates conflict and violence. Literature, because it offers a wide range of topics, experiences, and perspectives, is a valuable forum for developing understandings and communication skills in peace and education.

5

Illustrations

Expressions through arts as well as language contribute to peace. Art communicates much about situations where peace might exist again. Illustrations activate the senses, touch the human spirit, stimulate imagination and are useful for therapy as well as for raising awareness. With imagination, in *The Color of Home* (Hoffman, 2002), Hassan, a Somali refugee, painted a picture of his former home without war violence there. His father used the picture to decorate the walls of their temporary abode, thereby cheering up the entire family during their displacement. Arts are crucial in promoting peace and educating youth. Learning about the arts, and through them, also advances language development and literacy.

The functions of artwork in literature for youth include: establishing setting, defining and developing characters, cultivating or extending plot, reinforcing text, diversifying viewpoints, as well as providing coherence. Artwork entices interaction with the literature that contains it, which enables learning, fosters aesthetic appreciation, and aids memory retention. Illustrations stimulate affect through feelings along with thoughts about the literature's contents. There are multiple feelings that visuals stimulate (Raggl & Schratz, 2004). These feelings are interactions from the personal experiences, identity, and nature of each individual with the illustrative contents. Presentation features, like the layout of the literature and the media it may include, influence feelings. Affect is a filter for learning (Friedman & Förster, 2010). Hence, literature that will stimulate positive affect can aid comprehension. Literature that stimulates strong negative feelings can cause retention of information in the memory. Discomforting literature, like stories that convey the horror of a tragedy, can be recalled longer than literature with less emotional effects. Affect is also a stimulant for creativity, which negative and positive feelings rouse (Bledow, Rosing & Frese, 2013). Use of arts after experiencing literature is a way for youth expression of their resulting feelings and perceptions of the presented contents.

Knowledge development occurs through interaction with illustrations in literature. Depictions can aid comprehension of story setting, character traits and roles as well as plot (Hibbing & Rankin-Erickson, 2003). Coherence is the understanding of ideas and events that illustrations support. Pictures present sequence and representation of terminology that youth may not yet comprehend. Illustrations can also stimulate different viewpoints, especially when they contradict what the text presents. These contradictions are sometimes purposeful, which promote critical thinking about the meaning and presentations in the literature. Peter Spier's (1978) book *Oh, Were They Ever Happy* has text that conveys pleasure and pictures that show what would not stimulate that feeling. The parents in the story come home and observe how their children messily painted many parts of the house after their babysitter did not arrive. The story features perspective variation, which is a skill youth need. Good illustrations support multicultural and other types of knowledge about populations and places that are unfamiliar to youth. Accurate depictions and stimulating techniques of illustration attract attention needed for development of social, artistic, and linguistic knowledge.

Illustrated literature is very useful in development of emergent and visual literacies (Arizpe & Styles, 2003). Visual literacy involves reading and writing images (Avgerinou &

Petterson, 2011; Rowsell, McLean & Hamilton, 2012). Skills formed in the early phase of literacy include print awareness, comprehension, and vocabulary (Fletcher & Reese, 2004). Language and literacy skills can simultaneously develop (Lonigan, Farver, Phillips, & Clancy-Menchetti, 2011). These coincide with development of artistic literacy—interacting with, interpreting, and creating art. For example, students can dramatically pose, walk, dance, or speak for showing the feelings of a character. Raising their awareness of how the body expresses feelings is a skill of conflict analysis. Identifying in illustrations and acting out feelings reinforces the development of vocabulary they need to learn and use. Learning the cues of feelings, which physical nuances of body language convey, builds understanding of nonverbal communication. Identifying the artistic techniques that express feelings is essential for understanding how the arts communicate.

Artistic literacy that illustrations support in youth literature is a tool for peace education. It includes understanding of art techniques and their uses in connection with peace. Artistic literacy involves reading artistic expression for identification of techniques and their effects. With these skills, youth can think about how the different ways that artists illustrate literature affect thoughts and moods. For example, how does the choice of illustration size, position, color, and use of line evoke feelings about it (Prior, Willson, & Martinez, 2012)? Facilitative questions include: *How do the illustrations stimulate your senses; make you hear, smell, taste, or feel some part of the context the literature presents? What part of the illustration activates your senses? Which of those help you feel peaceful or not?* The latter question supports identification of situations in which there is a need for or evidence of peace development. The interaction of the artist with the individuals who experience the illustration supports self-awareness (Fohfink, 2012). The importance of inner processes in pursuit of peace highlights a crucial role that the arts play in the education of youth.

Illustrations in the literature that youth observe mirror relations and experiences in their own lives, when young people can recognize those representations. Regardless of cultural differences, people often have similar types of conflicts. While the common sort of conflicts humans have are universal and relatable to many people, the representation of their identities and communities aids youth engagement with literature (Hicks, 2002). The regions, cultures, and symbols that the illustrations or book design include help youth connect with the literature. This connection aids recognition of contexts for their involvement in peace. Illustrating the literature contents in their own lives is one way to help youth see those connections. When asked about how arts affected learning, a student replied, "I learned about my community and it made me want to help" (The New York Department of Education, 2010, p. 33). While awareness of places for peace work in a community is worthwhile, youth need knowledge about the various perceptions of that place that others have and the needs discernable in each perspective of it. Critical literacy engages youth in perspective diversification.

Critical literacy involves youth in identification and consideration of multiple viewpoints of literature's content (Hagood, 2002). The goal is recognition of conflicts and their ideas on possible responses to those problems (Stribling, 2009). Readers think deeply about representations in the literature and proactively respond to them after they analyze a conflict it reveals. Evidence of social injustice, for example, through bad representation of a particular population prompts proactive responses. Balancing or replacing that literature with good representations of the group is a needed action. Critical thinking goes beyond representation of populations to techniques of visual culture (Duncum, 2005). Youth identify the cultural foundations of the artwork used in illustrations and the appropriateness of those representations for bias, authenticity, accuracy, and other aspects brought to their attention. They can create their own illustrations for the subject matter in the literature to render improved expressions of the presented cultures and situations. Multiple literacies, involving the contents and ways students are literate outside of school, are essential for engaging all youth in reading and analysis of conflict ((Barton, Hamilton, & Ivanic, 2000; Mahiri, 2004; Tiernery, 2008; Zenko et al, 2009). As a tool for communicating and a way of responding to conflict, the arts have indispensible roles in peace development (Schank & Schirch, 2008).

Construal of Peace

Interpretation by youth of illustrations reveals the various ways they identify peace. Depending on their experiences in life, they will have their own ways of recognizing contexts of conflict. One person sitting alone somewhere may represent peace to one child where another person sees the lack of social interaction with others as a conflict. Culture, life events, and individual preferences shape the perspectives of an illustration, in addition to their observable techniques that affect viewers' responses. These various perspectives are rich resources for intrapersonal and interpersonal understanding. Hence, it is worthwhile to have youth communicate together with others about perceptions of peace and conflict, which the literature stimulates.

Youth can communicate about viewpoints through discussions, writing, and their own illustrations in graphic or performing art. Use of circle time as a large group, learning center with a small group, or partners are formats for those discussions (Pranis, 2005). Composing or selecting songs that represent a situation is an artistic response to the meaning of illustrations. In the same vein, creating skits in which youth can demonstrate how a context is peaceful taps creativity as a mode of interpreting illustrations. The engagement with the arts as a response to illustration demonstrates the importance of creativity and diversity for the interpretation of meaning.

When different genres of arts are the means for expressing perceptions, youth can discern diversity of communications styles as well as viewpoints.

Selection of the literature for use in arts analysis must be inclusive. Art educators in areas of conflict and violence can find a variety of representations for all populations in the region. Meeting this challenge entails incorporation of literature from many sources and graphic art outside of literature for analytically reading. Critical analyses of art facilitated by teachers in areas of violence have included three processes: therapeutic, broadening the gaze of the "other," and deconstructing the imagery of the "other" (Cohen-Evron, 2005). The methods range from helping students express their own experiences with violence and resulting trauma to deconstructing and expanding their conceptions of oppositional people—those perceived as enemies. Conceptions of the "other" are not limited to contexts of observable violence. Hence, literature and art that helps youth recognize what triggers that notion in their minds is worthwhile in peace education.

Ideas and feelings that youth have about peace, conflict, and war are functions of developmental, cultural, and situational factors (Raviv, Bar-Tal, Koren-Silvershatz, & Raviv, 1999). Age determines cognitive development. As youth mature, their thinking expands beyond a self-focused viewpoint to inclusion of others' experiences in the context of conflict. Cultural influences social knowledge that a group's history and living conditions shape. A collective memory of violence the group may have influences its youth's thinking patterns. Situational factors like direct observation of violence and peace development affects the conceptions youth form in response to literature and art. All of these factors need consideration when helping youth form their conceptions of peace.

Role of Youth Literature

Useful for construing peace are perceptions of self and the "other" that youth have while observing illustrations. Hence, literature about people who are different from as well as similar to readers is peace curriculum. In *What a Family* (Isadora, 2006), readers see how family members have many different racial characteristics across generations, along with their common traits. In addition to showing how those different traits comprise one family, the book features each member on a family tree and provides terminology for their placements (e.g., twin second cousins once removed). Peace as acceptance of diverse characteristics is important to youth who typically acquire through observations in their early years biases and prejudice. Very needed for counteracting bias and fostering pluralism are images of diversity as commonplace aspects of life. One bias youth typically learn through their socialization is gender differentiation, which is the root of sexism. The book *Are You a Boy or a Girl* (Jiménez, 2000) presents a young female suffering from criticism for doing "boy things." "Her mama took a deep breath and said, "You'll never be a girl like other girls and you'll never want to. Right now it's hard because too many people don't know about girls like you" (p. 13). The mother explains how throughout time there have been children who do activities that were not the same as others. She then reassures, "And when you know that and you're all grown up, you'll know that you can do anything you want to. And that's the best way to live" (p. 15). Illustrations of distinctly different people harmoniously doing activities demonstrate interpersonal peace.

Harmonious Living

Illustrations can depict harmony with self, others, and the environment. People who experience harmony adjust to their livable circumstances and work together for making needed improvements. The Earth Charter promotes collaboration for ecological as well as social harmony. Its principals include:

1. Respect Earth and life in all its diversity.
2. Care for the community of life with understanding, compassion and love.

3. Build democratic societies that are just, participatory sustainable and peaceful.
4. Secure Earth's bounty and beauty for present and future generations.

(Earth Charter Initiative, 2014, para 6)

The commitment to social and ecological harmony brings into view everything that comprises a situation.

Harmonious living reflects inner and outer processes. The interactions in those domains benefit from a clear purpose and awareness that life naturally presents challenges in the form of conflict. Constructive response to conflict within the self as well as with others are purposeful processes that can be taught in school and other places (Johnson & Johnson, 2010). Peace Pilgrim explained one step in that process;

> Relinquishment of the feeling of separateness. All of us, all over the world, are cells in the body of humanity. You are not separate from your fellow humans, and you cannot find harmony for yourself alone. You can only find harmony when you realize the oneness of all and work for the good of all (Pilgrim, n. d., p. 22)

A metaphor for global harmony is the human body. This image considers each nation like one part of a global body (Mercieca, 2011). Each part working in cooperation with other parts sustains the health of humanity. When segments of the body fail to cooperate, there is sickness and unnecessary suffering. This comparison of one living body with all of humanity demonstrates the crucial role that individuals and each nation have in bringing about well-being through harmony.

Visuals for showing youth components of harmony can include individuals, humans together, and other groups of life in nature. Interpretation of individuals doing their inner work for peace can be identified across types of illustrated literature. Explanations of that inner work reveal what each viewer thinks about the personal processes that support harmony. Awareness of that thinking supports discussion about the known and less-familiar process. For example, one might ask, "How is that person managing the inner voice? Does it appear that negative thoughts are happening or does it look like positive thoughts are a conflict response? How do you think those positive thoughts will help those involved in the conflict be healthier?

Role of Youth Literature

Conversion of lifestyles for social and ecological harmony is a goal, especially in prosperous regions where human waste of resources and pollution are very evident. Literature that illustrates such conversion plants the seeds of awareness needed for growing that movement toward peace. Interesting to those who are unfamiliar with them, as well as informative, are illustrations of sustainability in regions where humans have been continually living with their local resources. This information addresses the need for recognizing the value of sustainable practices that indigenous populations have maintained.

Images of children with different cultural and physical characteristics, along with biodiversity in nature, convey a message of interconnectedness in the *Our Big Home: An Earth Poem* (Glaser, 2000). Grounded in herstory, *Aani and the Tree Huggers* (Atkins, 2000) shows how deforestation in northern India prompted a girl's proactive response. Aani bravely wrapped herself around one of the trees to communicate the importance of saving them for the nearby people and the animals. Showing how youth can be active without risking their safety is *Compost Stew, An A to Z Recipe for the Earth* (Siddals, 2010). Its illustrations demonstrate scenes made from recycled and pasted paper that show the process of composting. Converting green waste to rich soil for growing plants can happen everywhere, even in urban dwellings. Exemplifying converted lifestyles is *The Green Mother*

Goose, Saving the World One Rhyme at a Time (Peck & Davis, 2011).

> Little Jack Horner changed bulbs in the corner,
> Replacing the old incandescents.
> Now the lamps on the sills cut his mama's high bills,
> 'Cause the lights are all compact fluorescents. (p. 14)

The roles of youth throughout the world are important to see for promoting the idea of global harmony. One role typically invisible in urban areas is *How Kids Help Feed the World* (Tate, 2013). While the book illustrates with photographs how youth around the world are active in food production, it also describes issues including genetic diversity and the use of pesticides. Additionally, the book stimulates thoughts about education—formal learning in schools versus learning at home and in the workplace about how to produce food. The collage illustrations by award-winning artist Susan Roth in *Listen to the Wind, The Story of Dr. Greg and Three Cups of Tea* (Mortenson & Roth, 2009), which she explicates in the book, illustrate the lives of youth in a Pakistani village. Their voices explain,

> Our families grow and gather the food we eat. Our mothers weave and sew the clothes we wear. We make our games and we make our toys. Before our school was built, we had lessons outside. We wrote with sticks in the ground. (p. 4)

Changing how the children lived there by constructing a school where they could study demonstrates the conflict of cultural change. The violence Malala Yousafzai (Yousafzai & Lamb, 2013) experienced while pursuing her education in Pakistan illustrates the conflict of educating girls where there is no consensus for that need.

Conflict Prevention

Illustrations in literature stimulate thoughts about past conflicts and prevention of future ones. Art presents problem sources, which aid in their identification and planning for proactive responses to the provocations that spur conflict. Art opens a window for viewing, sensing, and thinking about situations. Art therapy aids people in perception of and preparation for response to conflict (Goldblatt, Elkis-Abuhoff, Gaydos, Rose, & Casey, 2011; Moon, 2012; Spier, 2010). Words cannot express all perceptions and feelings. It is known that "pictorial representations constitute at least a rudimentary form of language (Kaplan, 2007, p. 99). Hence, facilitating awareness through art has become a method of conflict prevention. For example, benefits of art therapy for young victims of incest included prevention of further harm (Carozza & Heirsteiner, 1982).

Illustrations help youth recall the situations that affected them and other people they observed. Observations of art can help them pinpoint the sources of their own feelings as well as those of the illustrated character in the literature. Even when their focus is on the feelings of the characters in an illustration, they can make a vicarious connection when they recognize those feelings from experience in their own lives. This connection is a catalyst for reflection by youth. That process should extend to analysis of those experiences for lessons learned. Whether or not youth openly connect the problem illustrated in the literature to their lives, an opportunity to reflectively respond to the illustrations literature includes is worthwhile for them. The lessons resulting from reflection involve youth in identification of conflict sources and thinking about possibilities for prevention. When they can reflect with others, their awareness of conflict sources and effects expands.

Collective reflection on illustrations can increase awareness about all three domains of conflict: intrapersonal, interpersonal, and systemic. Communicating through words or artistic expression about many types of conflict situations brings needed attention to otherwise unrecognized contexts for prevention work. For example, awareness of inner conflicts such as anti-social dispositions that youth may have acquired is a response to related illustrations (Lee, 2013). With awareness of a propensity to make assumptions about, misunderstand, or feel unfriendly toward certain people, self-work can begin by changing those thoughts and responses. Identification of how perspectives are colored by experiences with race involves work with all three domains of conflict. For example, how does a scene depicting facilitation of reconciliation between people of different races look to students whose experiences have been differently affected by racism? Development goals for learning can be displayed during reflection for thinking about individual or group skills. Table 5.1 is a simple rubric for that use. It can be adapted for evaluation of skill development with any of the components of peace education: construal of peace, harmonious living, conflict prevention, avoidance and repair of harm, fulfillment of needs, and social and legal justice.

Role of Youth Literature

Artists, both graphic and performing, have been proactive in preventing conflicts as well as responding to them. They communicate about situations, which raises awareness and even brings people together. Whether they bring attention to a structural conflict widely observed or the experience of one person, artists have been instrumental in preventing further

Table 5.1   Skill evaluation

Skill	Opportunity	Developing	Evident
Conflict Prevention	Student might: Confirm an example of a prevention opportunity.	Student can: Identify an example of a prevention opportunity.	Student can: Suggest one or more prevention strategies.
Repair of Harm	Confirm an example of harm repair.	Identify an example of harm repair.	Suggest one or more ways to repair harm.

conflict and violence. The paintings that illustrate *Rent Party Jazz* (Miller, 2001) demonstrate this role of arts in conflict prevention. In addition to the story it tells about avoiding eviction after the loss of work, the book offers a brief history of rent parties to support people in financial crises. The harm avoided by raising funds needed during hard times through performances and donation of graphic arts is an accomplishment for which artists deserve more recognition.

Avoidance and Repair of Harm

Youth can learn identification in illustrations of harms that need to be avoided in the pursuit of peace. Additionally, they should pinpoint repair efforts that follow after harm. These orientations toward avoidance and repair are important for people of all ages, especially for those who lack the habit of thinking from other perspectives. Interaction with illustrations can provide awareness about harm to anything. With greater levels of maturity, youth can think critically about multiple causes of harm, possibilities for avoiding it and repair responses.

Youth learn about repair work in all three domains of conflict. Extremely important is knowledge of self-healing methods that people in different situations and cultures use. Since the inner processes may be more difficult to discern than physical activities, there is a need for communication about them. Discussion about the intrapersonal and structural processes people and other forms of life use to repair reveals perceptions how those processes. Those shared insights display not only thinking capabilities but also aspects of the repairs that may not have occurred to other observers of the illustration.

There is no consensus on the value of repair efforts. While efforts to accomplish restoration may seem sincere and effective in one viewpoint, others will see if differently. A humanistic viewpoint sees processes like official forgiveness and reconciliation as a healing response to structural violence, while a postmodern perception can discern an agenda of political reconstruction (McGonegal, 2009). Deconstructing reconciliation art, for example, though an indigenous lens reveals an emphasis on whiteness (Nicoll, 2004). Psychological conditions also affect repair efforts. Research found that levels of trust determine responses to repair efforts characterized by empathy (Nadler & Liviatan, 2006).

Critical analysis of human reaction to art emphasizes the importance of not pushing reasoning as a response (Morton, 2001). While youth express in words or arts their perceptions of an illustration, they should not be forced to rationalize those responses. Communication customs differ. Expression of personal perceptions does not feel comfortable to some for psychological as well as normative reasons. The manner of perceptions may include direct or indirect responses, depending on the cultural norms. Several cultures use storytelling and art as a way of indirect description of conflict and harm. Also, explanations can be difficult depending on skill levels of youth. Consequently, expression of awareness should be accommodating and feel comfortable. The climate of those interactions influences them. It is important to build a supportive milieu for communication about perceptions of art. The advice of Jean Paul Lederach (2005), a peace educator, to his students is to focus their peace thoughts on a picture, not words, for its description. That directive attends to their comfort while they are thinking about violence and peace.

Role of Youth Literature

Stories about how people protected and helped each other when faced with violence have multiple levels of use. While they convey the value of proactively responding to conflict, the avoidance and repair methods are suitable for critical analysis. The nonfiction account in *The Greatest Skating Race, a World War II Story from the Netherlands* (Borden, 2004) of how a Dutch boy skated endangered children to safety illustrates bravery and perseverance. However, his lie to the German soldiers who interrogated him on the journey is useful for critical thinking about means of avoiding harm. Youth can consider the impact of a lie on the liar as well as others. The childhood account of Archbishop Desmond Tutu learning to express forgiveness demonstrates the impact of communication on inner peace. The illustrations show deep emotions in *Desmond and the The Very Mean Word* (Tutu & Abrams, 2013) and how his retaliation with a mean word prolonged his unhappiness. He then understood the explanation of his mentor Father Trevor that retaliation hurts everyone and a way to heal is through forgiveness. After young Desmond apologized for his own use of a mean word, he felt stronger, braver, taller, and freer. Once Desmond was relieved of his inner turmoil, he felt "as if he could embrace the whole world in his outstretched arms" (p. 27).

While the children in *Play Lady* (Hoffman, 1999) do not express forgiveness, because they first have a desire for justice through arrest of the vandals who damaged the lady's garden and trailer, they get relief from repair of her little home. This book illustrates more than restoration after an intimidation crime. It shows participation of disabled and racially diverse families working together to immediately fulfill a need. The text in two languages additionally conveys the value of multilingualism, which enriches peace development. Concepts that are not transliterated demonstrate the need for multiple languages in fulfillment of needs.

Fulfillment of Needs

Illustrations stimulate sensations that are pathways to identification of needs. Awareness of artistic expression as a tool for recognition of needs resulted with purposeful uses of illustrations. Youth interaction with artistic expression encompasses spirituality, identity clarification, healing, and imagination. All of these processes are aspects of peace education.

Spirituality is a component of holistic education. Holistic education strives for well-being through cultivation of youth's physical, cognitive, and spiritual development (de Souza, Francis, O'Higgins-Norman, & Scott, 2010). In her analysis of the learning needs that children have, physician Maria Montessori (1992) identified the spiritual and practical-life experiences that balance cognitive development. Through secular education, Montessori's pedagogy cultivates spirituality and physical coordination by interaction with beautiful objects and images. While beauty affects the soul, children learn to more carefully handle exquisite objects, thereby improving their physical skills in the practical life component of Montessori education. They learn to pour rice, and then liquid, in beautiful crystal pitchers the do not want to break. Waldorf pedagogy incorporates art across the curriculum through humanism. Students learn about spiritual practices around the world, including multiple religions and indigenous traditions. Cross-cultural understanding that Montessori's and Waldorf's approaches cultivate optimally occurs through direct experience by youth (Waldorf Worldwide, 2014).

Identity clarification happens through interaction with literature and its illustrations. Reflections of the self that illustrations and text present can happen when literature provides a mirror for youth. Geneva Gay (1999) explains that literature enables understanding of the individual within a culture; the intra-ethnic as well as inter-ethnic experiences that shape identity. When self and intra-group concepts have been harmed by encounters with misrepresentation in literature, underrepresentation in school curriculum, social discrimination, or other factors, there is a need for repair of those conceptions (Ferrara, 2004). History, which under- or misrepresents people of an "out-group," negatively affects conceptions of that population (Korstelina, 2013). The more generalized a group is in an historical presentation the more they can be viewed as an enemy in dichotomies of "us and them" (Bahador, 2012). Useful for demonstrating unity are depictions that show the commonalities of people, in spite of their cultural differences. For example, artist Fabrica (2007) shows images in the minds of females in different regions, one being a war zone, revealing their similarities while contrasting their realities. Images of violence in the mind demonstrate a place for mental peace. The many forms of bibliotherapy reflect the need for healing from harm done to the identity and other psychological conditions that youth evidence.

Bibliotherapy encompasses several ways of helping youth fulfill their own needs. The influence of intrapersonal well-being on all aspects of one's life rationalizes use of illustrations for that accomplishment. Youth who have formed social biases need repair of their mental habits. Those who are objects of such biases benefit from literature and images that positively frames them. Gavigan and Kurtts (2011) explain how use of literature can promote acceptance and understanding of individual differences. They provide, in addition to strategies for those accomplishments, a bibliography of youth literature about special needs. The list includes specific examples of stories addressing Asperger, autism, Down syndrome, epilepsy, physical disabilities, attention disorders, etc.

Addressing needs with literature that has useful illustrations for therapy happens in deliberate processes: pre-reading, reading, responding in an extension activity, and follow-up (Cook, Earles-Vollarath, & Ganz, 2006). Response activities can include the students' own artistic expressions as well as journaling, forming questions, and analyzing their perceptions of the contents. Throughout these processes, interaction with youth reveal their perceptions and needs. Their need to cope with fear and their realistic, or not, conceptions of mortality will be evident when illustrations stimulate those important topics (Nicholson & Person, 2003). Research on how children think about death evidenced developmental stages in understanding the permanency of death. Additionally, it linked exposure to media violence with death-aversion deficiency (Fadul, 2008). This information underscores the importance of helping youth understand mortality and cope with their emotions when thinking about potential to permanent harm.

While response to illustrations can open up these spaces for topics that have been very quiet in schools, it is important to not use those openings for preaching values. In a list of recommendations for using books about homosexuality, Vare and Norton (2004) explain, "If books are overloaded with messages, bibliotherapy may result in didacticism or a modern form of Puritanism" (p. 191). Illustrations best depict possible solutions to problems that youth can consider. These depictions may stimulate the imagination, which is a crucial for picturing peace.

Imagining ways to meet needs can be stimulated through observation of illustrations. Youth can think about how the depictions show possibilities for providing essentials. They can also imagine other ways and express those in their art or words. Maxine Greene identified the importance of *Releasing the Imagination* (1995). In recognition of the role visioning has in peace history, educators use it for lessons about future as well as current challenges (Bertling, 2013; Boulding, 2000).

Role of Youth Literature

Youth create images in their minds when told about a situation. They incorporate in those images realities of their current lives. Families who have immigrated share with their children descriptions of their homeland. This sharing addresses the longing for home that people experience after leaving and passing on culture to their children. In *Faraway Home* (Kurtz, 2000) the father shares stories with his daughter about his childhood in Ethiopia. These help his daughter in a very different homeland imagine that lifestyle and carry on part of it. This connection relieves her concern when he must return to Ethiopia. The mental images she has of being there help her feel connected to him. This story is cogent for all youth whose parents must leave them and go to a far away place, as well as for children of immigrants.

The images of racial integration and nonviolence Dr. Martin Luther King Jr. cultivated during his outspoken pursuit of peace inspired many people. The book *Sit-In, How Four Friends Stood Up by Sitting Down* (Pinkney, 2010) provides artistic illustrations along with an actual photograph of the student's activism and even a civil rights' timeline. The illustrations exaggerate the food at the Woolworth lunch counter in Greensboro where whites had a full lunch and the youth had nothing for their simple order of coffee and a donut. By breaking the rule of racial segregation, their defiance filled a need for equal rights that people young and old, "black" and "white," subsequently responded to with their own sit-ins across the United States. The arts reinforce acts of civil disobedience as well as provide support for those who can positively answer the question in the popular song "Have you been to jail for justice?" (Feeney, 1998). While experiencing jail for his protests, Dr. Martin Luther King Jr. wrote about the need to end war (Feeman, 1967). Meanwhile, conscientious objectors to military service went to jail for their refusal of participation in war. The film *Muhammad Ali's Greatest Fight* portrays that widespread response to war as experienced by one famous athlete (Fish, 2013). *The Enemy, a Book About Peace* (Cali & Bloch, 2009) simply illustrates the vulnerability and humanity of soldiers with a desire to end war. When many people proactively responded to injustice and other structural problems without violence, they averted war (Steves, 2010).

Social and Legal Justice

The notion of social and legal justice is a product of vision. In the field of education, it is a curricular topic and a goal for providing all students with cultural representation and relevant lessons. It responds to the structural constraints that hold back youth whose lives lack the privileges that propel others successfully through schools. The theme of justice through equal opportunities and representation for all learners is explicit. Youth glean from that pursuit the interest in societal and individual peace that they as well as adults have had. Social and legal justice also encompasses the rights of teachers for facilitating these accomplishments. Illustration of the ways different people have actively pursued justice gives youth access to an historical record that is proportionally missing in the mainstream curriculum. Hence, literature that features images of how people moved on this path to peace fills a curricular need. Teachers and librarians find ways to fit this topic in the exposure to literature that youth have.

Fitting the topic of social justice into the lessons is easier when multiple forms of literature and student writing constitute curriculum (Singer, 2006). While educational standards must anchor the lessons teachers provide, there is a clear need for showing where social justice fits with those instructional recommendations. Hence, a body of literature that identifies that fit advances peace education. There is recognition of the fit in language arts, literacy, and social studies (Agarwal-Rangnath, 2013). Many forms of arts are useful in facilitation of multicultural and gender-inclusive representation. These depict human diversity, especially students' communities, families, and realities. They enable presentation in multiple subject areas of current as well as past conflict and peace situations (Walling, 2006). Identifiable in literature illustrations and visual media are social problems like consumerism—the commercial past time of shopping for gratification. Consuming violence through media and spectatorship is another conflict that youth can analyze and proactively address (Möller, 2013).

Mocking up possibilities for social and legal justice in response to conflict raises awareness through visual arts and provides rehearsal for civic action. People perform skits or tableaus of current conflict and then show ways they might be transformed for facilitation of justice. Theater is especially useful for identifying students' perceptions of an historical or current context. There is a need for age-appropriate images when teaching about horrific events.

To avoid psychological harm and build hope, there is a need for careful selection of literature that shows how people suffered from and proactively responded to systemic conflict and violence (Chen & Yu, 2006). Resources that review books for education about justice and other aspects of peace enable matching of age-appropriate literature. A dependable resource on the Internet has been the Jane Addams Peace Association (2014) that provides descriptors of all the books it lists in several categories of peace development.

Role of Youth Literature

The power of individual expression in response to injustice has been a catalyst for social and legal change, in addition to a means of coping with structural conflict. *Sojourner Truth's Step-Stomp Stride* (Pinkney, 2009) colorfully illustrates the life of this escaped slave's storytelling in her work as an abolitionist and suffragette. Children can appreciate the bravery of her long walks around a nation that legalized capture of fugitive slaves. The effects of her talks, including prevention of reactive violence when the Fugitive Slave Law passed, abolition, and support of the women's rights, may inspire youth to speak out about the injustice they recognize in their society. The illustrations of *Dolores Huerta, A Hero to Migrant Workers* (Warren, 2012) show her aging throughout the long struggle for safe working conditions and a living wage that farmworkers needed. It additionally exemplifies her work to overcome ongoing classism and sexism. The pictures in *Crossing Bok Chitto: A Choctaw Tale of Friendship and Freedom* (Tingle, 2006) illustrate the interactions of slaves and Native Americans living without human rights in the United States. The value of storytelling this book demonstrates is clear, especially in response to the underrepresentation of Native Americans and their assistance to slaves escaping inhumane oppression. Healing from oppression does not happen in one lifetime. The biography of Japanese American Alice Sumida demonstrates the role of beauty in the recovery process. In *Music for Alice* (Say, 2004) youth see how recovery from internment during World War II occurred through her hard work in the creation of a flower farm and her love of music.

Questions to Consider for Illustration through Youth Literature

From Evaluation Criteria for Youth Literature in Peace Education Copyright Candice C. Carter and Shelly Clay-Robison

1. Do the illustrations coincide well with the text?
2. Do the illustrations reinforce the plot and skills, or are they ambiguous?
3. Do the illustrations overwhelm the lessons and skills being taught?
4. Do the illustrations avoid stereotypes of "minority" groups?
5. Do the illustrations depict certain characters as weak members of society?
6. Are the illustrations of different ethnic groups realistic and express individuality?
7. Do members of an ethnic group look exactly like one another?
8. Are illustrations or photographs contemporary?
9. Do the images portray characters who engage in peaceful behaviors?
10. Do the illustrations compliment and enhance the presented peace skills?

Summary

Illustrations exemplify the role of arts in knowing and being. They communicate much more than words can say. Effects of artwork in literature range from stimulation of questions and facilitation of understanding to responsive expression through art. During consideration of how artwork affects dispositions and knowledge, youth learn of their subjectivity. They discover how visual techniques influence observers. This is the seed of critical literacy. Seeing illustrations from more than one viewpoint mirrors the analysis process needed in peace development. Multiple ways of looking at a problem are essential to recognizing the unmet needs that were revealed. While considering sources of problems that they discern in illustrations and shared responses to those depictions, youth learn to examine intrapersonal, interpersonal, and structural domains of conflicts. The arts provide a way for expressing their perceptions. Hence, youth need opportunities to create art as well as observe it. The history of art's role in pursuits of peace is crucial knowledge. Young people deserve awareness of how artists communicate about conflict and peace. That realization can motivate their lifelong observation of and participation in artistic expression.

6

Conflict

Conflict is a key to opening the peace door. It unlocks the entrance to opportunities. Entry into the conflict room enables problem analysis and response. Conflict work occurs in multiple domains. Those include self-work, engagement with others, and collective efforts to bring about changes needed in the accomplishment of peace. The first domain of conflict work is internal. Self-work is the threshold to the peace door. The decision about how to respond to conflict is individual work. Recognition of one's own needs, that negative emotions and thoughts reveal, supports identification and analysis of conflict. That work starts in the mind and progresses from internal to external interactions.

The second domain of conflict work exists in dealings with others and the environment. In this aspect, the relations between people and with everything else in their environment determine peace. Working through conflict for the optimal condition of everyone and everything that a problem affects is a peace process. The way that people respond to each other and their environment influences the outcome of their efforts.

Working together in an organized approach to a problem is the third domain of conflict work. Collective effort in response to conflict has been crucial for dealing with structural problems in an organization, society, and even across nations. This typically involves public efforts such as demonstrations and improvement activities by many people who work together or in concert at different locations. The pursuit of peace involves effort in all three domains of conflict. When conflict is widespread, such as structural problems like discrimination, people have to work on their own mental states, relations with others, and also organize for collective action. While conflict exists as inner feelings, its management can prevent or reduce a problem with others. Likewise, management of conflict between individuals and groups can avoid systemic problems that affect many people.

It is worthwhile to keep these domains in mind when selecting and using literature. Youth literature must reveal how people think about peace and respond to conflict with intrapersonal, interpersonal, and structural processes. Unfortunately, there is a lack of literature that fully describes the intrapersonal processes of conflict work. Additionally, more stories about collective action of people that avoided violence in response to widespread conflict would enhance peace education.

Construal of Peace

Conflict is the core of literature. It presents problems that reveal the challenges of existence as a living or nonliving component of our universe. People, especially adults, have different ways of thinking about peace according to the time and place of a conflict. The context of the situation they are in, along with their frame of mind shaped by culture and psychological condition, influences their conceptions of peace. When they have exposure to or immersion in direct violence, they think more about peace as the absence of destruction and harm. While adults construe peace in several different ways, research reveals that children around the world develop common patterns of thinking.

Children typically think about peace as social relations with others and enjoyable activities. As they think about conflict, the condition of those relations brings to mind well-being or harm. Research on the conceptions of youth about peace has most often connected that construct to war. A review of literature on the conceptions of peace found that children described the following ideas: social activities, absence of quarrels, and absence of war (Hakvoort & Hagglund, 2001). While research on children's conceptions of peace did include the concept of war with peace, the findings also identified a relationship between peace and children's thoughts about enjoyable activities, "Peace is hearing my cat purring" (Sunal, Kelley & Sunal, 2012). It is clear that children and youth do construe peace in all three domains of conflict, whether or not they can discern intrapersonal, interpersonal, and structural contexts of peace. Instruction that enables their identification and analysis of peace in all three domains portends toward their skill development across them.

Role of Youth Literature

Comparison of the different ways people construe peace is a cross-cultural learning experience for students. In that activity, youth can recognize the commonalities of humans across locations regardless of their cultural differences. In addition, they discover how people respond proactively to conflict regardless of mental and physical disabilities (Gervay, 2004). In reading about the pacifism and social activism of Helen Keller, students find examples of her work in all three domains of conflict (Helen Keller Museum, 2010). Overcoming the conflicts she experienced as a deaf and blind person was a foundation for the interpersonal and collective actions she took throughout her life. Her experiences are inspirational to others who promote peace activism in contexts of violence. Although at this writing there is no biography for youth featuring Helen Keller's peace work, other literature describes youth proactively responding to conflicts.

An example set in Afghanistan illustrates the decisions of a female who violates the prohibitions in her society so she can provide food to her family. In *The Breadwinner* (Ellis,

2001), Parvana changes her appearance to that of a male after deciding she must overcome the restrictions that the Taliban have mandated for female activities outside the home. To her, peace is caring for one's family in the face of political and cultural conflict that may have deadly consequences. Stories that address intrapersonal work demonstrate the critical aspect of bravery and summoning courage. Louise Diamond describes in her book *The Courage for Peace* (1999) structural conflicts that she faced and the self-work she did that supported her pursuit of peace in her family, society, and between nations. Organizations that try to prepare youth for that work focus on strengthening capacities like bravery when facing dangerous situations. For example, Aware Girls (2012) aimed at development of a Youth Peace Network where there is evidence of extremism. Structural problems that impede equal rights for people with different characteristics, such as disability, race, gender, and sexual orientation, require multidimensional conflict work. It is necessary to use the examples of that work in different books when an author does not present them in the same story.

In *Mr. Lincoln's Way* (Polacco, 2001) the title character explains to the student repeating discriminatory statements he has learned at home that "sometimes people get trapped in their thinking." (p.10). Mr Lincoln, the school principal, gently helps the boy who has been repeating those statements to insult peers at school in seeing a need for change in one's mind and habits. The boy's work to manage his inner turmoil resulting from conflicting norms in school and home involves his promise to stop insulting others. Treating oneself well along with others is an important aspect of intrapersonal peace that literature can present. The good feelings in life, which support conflict work, characterize construal of peace. *What Does Peace Feel Like* (Radunsky, 2004) illustrates this with sight, sound, smell, taste, and touch. "What does Peace feel like? Like hugs your friends give you when you cry"(p. 11). The incorporation of physical senses for perceiving peace is an experience that youth in every culture can do. Construing how that might be differently done advances with the book *Can You Say Peace?* (Katz, 2006). It translates the word peace and depicts across two large pages the context in which each translation would be used. The book concludes with, "No matter how we say it, we all want peace" (p. 26). Beyond perceptions that aid identification of peace and terms for that universal concept are situational illustrations in the book *If Peace Is...* (Baskwill, 2003). Each page illustrates with a short rhyme a depiction of an action that might constitute peace. "If peace is candle, I'll light one each night. If peace is a hand, I'll hold on so tight" (pp. 1–2). The author also explains peace: "Peace is a promise we make one another to love and protect and to care for each other" (pp. 11–13). In *A Little Peace* (Kerley, 2007) photographs illustrate global contexts for accomplishing peace. The idea that people should live in harmony with nature as well as each other has come full circle, from indigenous heritage to contemporary efforts and future plans.

Harmonious Living

Harmonious living for peace involves nondestructive response to conflict. People work together to identify and understand needs that conflict evidences. After identification of needs, they collaborate for fulfillment of life essentials. That response highlights the desire for things that are not necessary. Literature helps students understand these processes when it presents characters who recognized the value of harmonious relationships with self and others. It can demonstrate the values that are supportive of harmonious interactions. The indirect orientation to those values allows students individual consideration of them. Indirect gleaning of values from storytelling and literature has been an enduring method of teaching. Indirect instruction pertaining to social problems has been more effective than direct methods in which students are told what they should think about other people. This phenomenon can be seen in the social behaviors of youth who do what they have seen in real life and the media. Countering antisocial behaviors learned from those observations is a tall task for teachers. Hence, literature has a crucial role in education for harmonious relations. Augmenting literature is instruction that helps youth collaboratively work with others.

There is widespread awareness that "interpersonal peace is an indispensible requisite for harmonious living in society" (Nair, n.d., p. 37). Self-awareness supports interpersonal peace when there is clarity about values that determine individual and group behaviors. Learning to live together in harmony involves experience with application of values. Education for harmony as an aspect of peace that aims "to strengthen the formation of values and abilities such as solidarity, creativity, civic responsibility, the ability to resolve conflicts by nonviolent means and critical acumen" (UNESCO Asia and the Pacific, 1998, p. 2). The value of all life forms, at least in the role of supporting well-being on earth, is apparent in sustainability curriculum. "Teacher Training for Learning to Live Together" provides lesson plans that promote international understanding and sustainability (Asia-Pacific Centre of Education for International Understanding, 2008). In a figure that differentiates negative and positive interdependence, Johnson and Johnson (2009) show that harmonious interaction aimed at mutual benefit is evidence of peace. The depiction uses distance to distinguish positive interdependence from discordant, hostile interaction aimed at differential benefit (p. 224). Literature that demonstrates benefits of a life in harmony with self, each other, and nature is useful for imparting the values that underlie positive interdependence.

Role of Youth Literature

How the characters in literature work through conflict to maintain or obtain harmony can support awareness of and ideas for enacting positive interdependence. While peace history is replete with a record of human cooperation in nonviolent response to conflict, fictional accounts also have instructional value. The efforts characters make to maintain harmony and the strategies they use, especially across time and cultures, support awareness of values and possibilities for their enactment.

In *The Best Eid Ever* (Mobin-Uddin, 2007), a young girl missing her parents who are away on their Hajj Pilgrimage finds helping refugee neighbors not only builds harmony in their new location, it fills the void of her loneliness. This book builds cross-cultural harmony with its illustration of an Eid celebration by Muslims in the United States and with the translation to English of the vocabulary it uses in other languages. How conflicts of humanity may escalate to spread violence is the topic of *Restoring Harmony* (Anthony, 2010). While the main character's family developed a sustainable lifestyle alone, her international trek in areas of violence to reach her grandfather involves the decision of shooting his captor. She does not carry out her threat to shoot the antagonist because he releases her grandfather. While the setting presents sustainability, the plot presents an opportunity to contemplate how the heroine might have accomplished her goal without threatening harm. The classic book *My Side of the Mountain* (Craighead, 2004), which was republished, features conflicts in two domains. The teenager, who feels a need for greater attention in his family, leaves them to live a year in the wilderness. After his year of living harmoniously with animals in the mountains, he has the inner peace to return to life with his family. Literature can demonstrate difficult challenges in prevention of conflict, like leaving one's family.

Conflict Prevention

Conflict is evident in negative emotions, relational discord, harm, or lack of sustainable living. The root of a conflict reaches down to an unmet need. People can dig down to the root of an existing conflict and they can plant the seeds of peace in caring relationships. Literature that demonstrates the potential for conflict and ways people prevent strife provides models that can help youth develop those skills. Additionally, literature that shows containment of an extant problem during the responses to the conflict has value in peace education.

Literature that reveals how characters reflect during conflict models a process that benefits people of all ages, whether or not they are thinking about a conflict. Description of reflective activities and revelations from contemplation by characters demonstrate worthwhile processes for all domains of conflict work. With instructional guidance, youth can identify the characters' own perspectives in a conflict. Their discourse about how one sees a situation in comparison to another evidences the analytical process that enables full examination of a conflict. Unawareness of others' viewpoints and unsatisfactory feelings hinders a sense of well-being and feeds the roots of the impending conflict. The insights to a problem conveyed by characters models efforts to understand. As mentioned before, modeling by characters of intrapersonal work for peace is curriculum for learning peace building. Building up existing peace is a continual task for humans to prevent violence as a response to conflict.

In the 1990s the term *conflict prevention* emerged to describe work done with international conflicts. It has multiple meanings to professionals and researchers of peace. First, it means identification and proactive response to the roots of potential conflicts. Another meaning used by international conflict workers is the prevention of violence in dispute resolution between nations. More recently, conflict professionals oriented the term towards early identification of a problem and careful response to it for the avoidance of its escalation (Ackermann, 2003). Provision of a quality education is prevention of conflict for individuals, groups, and their society (Wedge, 2008). Examination of armed conflicts reveals the vulnerability of schools for involvement because "students, teachers and administrative staff may be targeted for intimidation, recruitment and indoctrination, and school premises are often damaged, destroyed or occupied by fighters" (Wedge, 2008, p. 6). As one means for avoiding violence in their society, it is crucial that people learn about conflict prevention and management. Youth can identify in literature problem prevention and avoidance of harm as a response to conflict.

Role of Youth Literature

Literature can illuminate conflict prevention in families and other relationships. It can also highlight human motivation to protect unknown people and the places humanity impacts. For example, how can humans anticipate life in outer space without violence when they encounter other life forms? How can their cooperation in space as well as on earth prevent harm to part or all of humanity? How might the prevention of violence in space be helpful? These questions are intended to stimulate literature development, as well as to support the use of existing texts. There is a need for literature that facilitates future thinking and planning for peace.

The challenge that the sheep in *Wild and Woolly* (Parker, 2005) face is connecting with each other as friends across the differences that divide them. The solution of the big horn and ranch sheep is to step outside their normal environment for overcoming the challenge of being together. While those steps felt uncomfortable because each was not accustomed to the other's terrain, they made adaptations that sustained their relationship. This book indirectly addresses the conflict of overlooking the potential for fulfilling relations across cultural borders. Friendships make creatures and people feel good. Positive feelings charge our creative batteries for shining the light on potential problems. *The Feel Good Book* (Parr, 2009) whimsically illustrates on every page one way that people feel good, "Sharing your treats feels good" (p. 15). It also shows how to reduce stress in the intrapersonal domain, it has several examples of feeling good with others.

The book concludes by asking the reader, "What makes you feel good?" Relieving stress before, during, and after conflict is an important strategy for improving well-being. Use of this book can expand to include discussion about how feeling good in the mind heals both the body and relationships during enjoyable activities together. Shared enjoyment relieves harm done to a relationship during conflict.

Avoidance and Repair of Harm

Evidence of conflict is a sign that there is a need to avoid harm or do repair from its effects. Monitoring negative emotions and thoughts about response to conflict is necessary work at the individual and group level. Awareness of feelings and analysis of relationships are important when thinking about conflict response. Relations with others affect both avoidance and repair efforts. Consequently, a focus on the quality of relations with others involved in the conflict and even those with whom one interacts daily is a primary goal in conflict work. Whether the task is immediate resolution of a conflict or transformation, humans need to look at relations with self and others. Conflict resolution is the short-term effort to solve a problem, while transformation of conflict involves long-term work that focuses on the roots of the problem. Social isolation, for example, is a conflict that can be resolved by making connections, while transformation of it addresses the causes, such as societal discrimination, low self-esteem, and effects of abuse at home or elsewhere. There is a need to both resolve the immediate conflict and also transforms the situations discerned in analysis of its root cause. Literature provides examples of how avoidance of harm during conflict and needed repair happens. The presentations in literature provide hope for youth grappling with conflict and its effects as well as ways in which the processes occur.

The use of restorative practices in schools varies. While these practices have been oriented toward discipline for the well-being of a school and its members, the processes involved have been useful for avoidance and repair of harm (Carter, 2012). The use of circles for discussion by all members of a class and the people outside of it who are connected in a conflict (Pranis, 2005) has been a helpful strategy. In *Circle in the Square: Building Community and Repairing Harm in School*, Riestenberg (2012) describes how circles enabled communication about conflict at all stages—prior to and after harm.

Role of Youth Literature

Dealing with the psychological detriments of social injustice can be very difficult and resulting in harmful response to self or others. Literature can show youth how people coped and avoided harm in those situations. Two stories about the Japanese American strife endured during the discrimination against and internment of these citizens around World War II demonstrate avoidance and repair of psychological harm. In *A Place Where the Sunflowers Grow* (Lee-Tai, 2006), a displaced Japanese American found drawing, and a new friendship in the internment camp helped her replace despair with the joy of a relationship. The sunflowers her mother managed to cultivate in the barren internment camp became symbols of hope. The ability to anticipate a better future kept the couple in *Music for Alice* (Say, 2004) working very hard throughout their lives together. After the death of her spouse, Alice realized their efforts together in the face of hardship sustained their relationshipand helped them survive and repair the harm done to them by political, economic, and social injustice. Alice's enjoyment of music through dance returned in her senior years while she reflected on her accomplishments in life. Finding the activity that relieves psychological and physical stress is an important aspect of peace for people of all ages. The relief of psychological and physical anxiety clears the mind and enhances its ability to create and think. Forgiveness is a means of relieving stress from harm. The book *Trouble in the Barker's Class* (De Paola, 2006) features the forgiveness of a new student in class who initially bullies her classmates. Her apology to them and their forgiveness of her follows the inquiry of one she bullied, "Why are you so nasty at school? Don't you like our class?" (p. 26). The proactive classmate who was the object of the bullying demonstrates interest in the offender and the desire to communicate in their new, albeit difficult, relationship. Finding out the reason for harm done in a conflict should lead to identification of unmet needs.

Fulfillment of Needs

Needs cannot be addressed before their identification. Literature can show youth processes that facilitate identification of needs. Additionally, it can show the creativity in problem solving and multiple means for accomplishing that are crucial responses to conflict. The needs that characters and their environment reveal in literature are very useful content for conflict analysis. Communication about those essentials and possibilities for providing them can occur through discussion, writing, and depictions by youth. Having terminology for expressing needs enables that communication.

Supporting the use of discourse about needs and their fulfillment is the Center for Nonviolent Communication. It offers multiple publications and online resources that can help people in many walks of life express their own needs and help others do that too. The Feelings Inventory at their website contains lists of words expressing peaceful and other frames of mind that people can use (Center for Nonviolent Communication, 2013a). Additionally helpful is the list of vocabulary in the Needs Inventory (Center for Nonviolent Communication, 2013b). In recognition of multilingual necessities, the organization sells learning aids in different languages and for multiple stakeholders in the education of youth. A document available on the organization's website presents a Nonviolent Communication Experimental Project in Primary Schools (Costetti, no date).

Analysis of conflict involves a look into deep culture, which is the core beliefs and values a group of people share. The skills of identifying value and belief differences in cross-cultural conflict are just as important as strategies for communicating across cultures (Oetzel & Ting-Toomey, 2013). Once the value in a conflict is evident, the need for enacting it and the opportunity can be created. Analysts of conflict resolution emphasize the importance of empathy for those who feel conflict (Marter, 2013). Literature that stimulates empathy has value for youth who work to identify unmet needs they can discern. "A person with an interdependent self-concept readily sees similarities with others and therefore may be more inclined to be empathic and forgiving" (Mayton II, 2009, p. 74). Hence, cultivating an awareness of interdependence in conflict and all situations portends towards empathy development.

Role of Youth Literature

The historical fiction by Eve Bunting reliably illustrates interdependence and need fulfillment. In her book *One Green Apple* (2006), the immigrant Farah is in need of connection and acceptance from her classmates in her new school, where she hears her homeland mentioned without the fondness she feels for it. In recognition of her need for connection, some of her classmates introduce themselves and smile at Farah. By the end of her first day with them, she recognizes that although she does not dress or speak like them, she will learn to fit in with them while expressing the culture she brought from her homeland. Fitting in with the linguistic culture of his one immigrant parent is the conflict the boy feels in *Cooper's Lessons* (Shin, 2004). His parent's frustration with Cooper's failure to speak his heritage language of Korean ends when he starts speaking it with a Korean store owner. This initiative brings respect to Cooper and his appreciation of his new bilingual skills. It also indicates his adjustment to a bicultural identity. A student's need for affirming the creed of nonviolence she has a Mennonite while she speaks to war veterans at her school assembly exemplifies the inner conflict youth can feel when faced with conflicting values. The student Rose in *A Piece of Forever* (Gugler, 2009) finds respectful support from a veteran for her promotion of peace. In *One Hen* (Milway, 2008), young Kojo asks for a loan in his village so he can invest in one hen. He receives and pays back the loan as well as saves enough money to pay for his education. He also helps his entire community by loaning money to families who can then afford to feed and educate their children as well as refund the loans Kojo makes to them. The book illustrates how making changes in the world can happen "one person, one family, one community at a time" (p. 31). Responding to structural problems like poverty takes initiative.

Social and Legal Justice

Conflict that entire populations experience indicates the potential for violence if members who suffer from lack of need fulfillment do not find harm-free ways for resolving the conflict. In addition to transforming how people feel about each other in systemic conflict, there is a need to address how individuals who sustain the injustice and those who suffer from it think about themselves. The ongoing condition of injustice can become normalized in the minds of people who live with it. They learn to accept advantages, like social privilege. At the same time, those who are the objects of that injustice may believe that they are less worthy of equal rights. Characteristic differences like gender, race, and ethnicity have been associated with lower self-concepts in environments of social and legal injustice. Hence, youth need exposure to literature that cultivates a desire for social equality and the right to legal justice for everyone. Additionally, they can obtain ideas and motivation for responding to structural conflicts from literature that presents processes. Carol Boston Weatherford (2005) quotes the store lunch-counter integration activists, historically known as the Greensboro Four, who demonstrate the maintenance of their self-conceptions along with their motivation for activism. "'We didn't like not having dignity and respect,' said Franklin McCain. 'I went out of the store feeling powerful'" (Weatherford, 2005, p. 28).

The feeling of power is central in conflict work. Everyone needs the power for fulfilling their needs in nonharmful ways. Instruction with a social justice-orientation highlights these two aspects of experiencing and responding to conflict: awareness of power differential and the feelings it causes. Enabling student to identify characters' feelings in a story and the conflicts that stimulate those emotions is a corollary for instruction that incorporates the real-life conflicts youth currently face (Christensen, 2009).

Preparation of curriculum for learning about social justice takes into account the realities of the students, their school, and society to render relevant lessons. Doing that work in mandatory standards- and test-oriented instruction invokes teacher feelings about their power for curriculum design. The process involves the self-awareness of the teachers as well as knowledge of their students' realities.

- Teachers see themselves as both responsible for and capable of challenging and altering an educational system that is not adequately serving large numbers of children, particularly poor children.
- Teachers challenge students to examine the world around them and encourage students to make change in their schools, communities, and world (Agarwal-Rangnath, 2013, p. 4).

In reflective research on his use of critical literacy, Woods (no date) found that his pupils connected literacy to their lives and possibilities for changing situations. His student Moses saw the literature in his kindergarten classroom dealt with conflicts associated with race and poverty that were aspects of his own life.

Role of Youth Literature

As a model of the self-work needed when living in the midst of structural conflict, *No Bad News* (Cole, 2001) shows how Marcus sees his neighborhood comprised as "bad news" because of many social problems. After his walk alone through the neighborhood on his way to purchase a haircut, his neighbors in the barbershop point out the good news in their neighborhood. One adult advises him, "Son, you can't see anything with your head held low. And you need to not only see the good news. You need to be the good news" (Cole, p. 25). Marcus changes his focus on the way home to notice all of the good things happening around him and he has an awareness of how he can control his perception of situations and his own response to them. In *Goin' Someplace Special* (McKissack, 2008), the author illustrates her discrimination experience with racial segregation and Jim Crow laws. She manages to control her frustration and sadness with a focus on getting to the special place that didn't allow racial integration in Nashville, Tennessee—the public library. Sustaining her trek alone to the library through unjust situations was the memory of her grandmother who explained, "You are somebody, a human being—no better, no worse than anybody else in this world. Getting' someplace special is not an easy route. But don't study on quittin', just keep walking straight ahead—and you'll make it" (McKissack, 2008, p. 26). The determination that people need in their proactive response to injustice has been crucial for responders to structural conflict, whether or not they were directly affected by it. Stories about how people with privilege worked to counteract it are also important for illustrating determination and other dispositions needed for resolving structural conflict. In *Emma's Poem, the Voice of the Statue of Liberty* (Glaser, 2010), the awareness of privilege and the lack of support from wealthy friends in aiding the underprivileged demonstrates the power of writing in response to poverty. Emma's poem about the plight of immigrants had a longer impact than the fundraising for them she did during her brief life.

Combining communication about social and legal injustice with collaboration while using culturally relevant literature are strategies for not only promoting critical literacy but also enhancing youth engagement in literacy instruction that would otherwise not motivate their involvement with the provided curriculum (Wood & Jocius, 2013).

Questions to Consider for Conflict Education through Youth Literature

From Evaluation Criteria for Youth Literature in Peace Education

Copyright Candice C. Carter and Shelly Clay-Robison

1. Does the literature present skills and tools for transforming conflict without the use of violence (physical or psychological harm)?
2. Does the literature facilitate multiple perspectives of a conflict?
3. Does the story investigate underlying causes of a conflict?
4. Does it give insight to the problem?
5. Does the literature reveal the process of enmity: an antagonist deserving violence?
6. Does the literature demonstrate or encourage reflection in response to conflict?
7. Does the literature demonstrate examination of feelings?
8. Does the literature demonstrate and encourage readers to engage in peace strategies?
9. Are the complexities of world peace evident?
10. Does the book promote behaviors known to transform and resolve conflict, or is it detrimental (Does it reinforce peace-promoting behaviors for ending conflict)?
11. Are conclusions believable and viable?
12. Is there a forced "happy ending"?
13. Is economic justice addressed?
14. Is social justice addressed?
15. Is environmental justice addressed?
16. Does the literature promote hope and foster futurism?

Summary

There are three peace-oriented responses to conflict. Pursuit of peace happens through: (1) self-work, (2) thoughtful interactions with others and the environment, and (3) group efforts that proactively respond to conflict. All three domains of conflict work can occur simultaneously. The concerted efforts are intrapersonal, interpersonal, and structural processes that prevent or respond to conflict. Although people think about peace in different ways, literature is useful for demonstrating the diverse ways people can work in the three domains. Youth learn that positive interdependence and efforts to meet needs are important in response to conflict. They anticipate the future and processes that will prevent as well as respond without harm to conflicts they identify. The concept of justice for all, human and other creatures, demonstrates the complexities of peace and situations for conflict work. Use of multiple perspectives for thinking about a conflict can occur with different pieces of literature on the same topic. Additionally, identification of techniques in the literature that promote enmity, one who deserves harm, is an important skill during conflict analysis. Ultimately, the use of literature for understanding and responding to conflict can foster reflection on problems youth face in their own lives.

7

Inclusive Peace Her/History

History is an interpretation of occurrence. It involves collection and analysis of information followed by description of the findings. Peace history focuses on events where there was a need for, or preserving an existing condition, of peace. It is the study of peoples' thoughts about and activities for the goal of accomplishing change (Cortright, 2008). *Herstory* is a term that emphasizes the purposeful inclusion of the female role in history. It features, among other processes, nurturing human connection across cultures and feminism (Schott, 1997). Herstory includes the female role in historical research on as well as their involvement in the studied occurrence (Alonso, 1995). Inclusive peace her/history incorporates this information. Comprehension of multiple meanings is possible with the inclusion of information about how different people experienced or perceived an event.

Clarification of what a situation meant to everyone involved aids in the analysis of a conflict. Use of multiple sources of information enables that clarification. Probing into the experiences of people with different characteristics and roles in an occurrence illuminates the needs that existed. Identifying and understanding desires of different people is a requisite skill for accomplishing conflict resolution. Without meeting all needs in a conflict, its root grows. Hence, learning with literature about different types of experiences and requirements is preparation for effective work with conflict in the pursuit of peace.

Youth can learn analysis of conflict through identification of its multiple meanings. They discern in the literature, and bring to it, diverse perspectives of the situations presented. Looking at a situation through different viewpoints than others expands their awareness. The ability to discern different ways of seeing the same situation aids their understanding of multiple needs. Youth learn distinction of perceptions that an analysis of a situation requires. Through practice with these skills, they can discern imbalanced history and then seek more information to reinterpret what happened (Woodward, 1989). In areas of cross-cultural violence, youth know there are multiple histories (Yogev, 2010). Respecting and legitimating the perceptions of "the other" in a society characterized by violence is a component of peace education, which educational standards prescribe (Carter, 2006). Educators who created standards for peace education responded to the increasing exposure youth have to violence through media, security work, military, gangs, and literature about violence that constitutes their curriculum. They need information about and opportunities for contemplating the pursuit of peace throughout the record of humanity.

Construal of Peace

Stories about the pursuit of peace demonstrate how people interacted in that process. Those accounts reveal what stimulated awareness of and proactive responses to the need for peace. A story about a teacher's conviction to nonviolence during wartime illustrates the role of commitment to harm-free conflict resolution (Boersema & Brown, 2006; Howlett & Howlett, 2008). Recognition and elimination of racism and sexism have been conceptions of peace that policies such as nondiscrimination rules as well as history reveal (Robinson, 2005). Stories about work towards hunger elimination and shelter for homeless people demonstrate the notion of peace as fulfillment of life-sustaining needs. Conceptions of peace through guaranteed rights of all adults and children are evident in the human rights policies of the United Nations. Analysis of such notions about peace evidences variation in support for pursuit of that condition. The lack of full ratification by the United States for the United Nations Convention on the Rights of the Child demonstrates this variation (United Nations, 2009). Historians initially focused their peace history on the topic of war (Curti, 1985). Until recent publications, history linked peace to accounts of war. Female historians expanded analyses of structural conflicts by bringing attention to factors such as gender empowerment (Björkdahl, 2012). Gender inequality is the root of unresolved conflicts in many contexts, including humanitarian relief (Olivius, 2011). The conditions of their lives affected peoples' ability to construe local and world peace. If the needs of females in a society were unmet, the society experienced more conflict and violence. Herstory is a record of female activism to address their needs, which affected their society as well as themselves. Students learn through literature how people eschewed violence.

Role of Youth Literature

In modern times, literature is the main mode used by teachers for history instruction. Hence, youth literature has an important role as curriculum. Information about how people construe peace has a use in all subject areas. The cross-curricular nature of social studies and language arts allows for inclusion of information from other disciplines. The information that youth read about in language arts, science, and history document technological innovations that have contributed to well-being. Humans need time for thinking about peace, across subject areas in school and other contexts of their lives.

The history of peace as a goal for humanity advanced in the last century following two world wars. In *Peace One Day*

(2005), Jeremy Gilley explains in prose, photos, and graphic art the challenges he faced in establishing One Day of Peace worldwide. His production of a film by that title, along with his personal request to world leaders, resulted with the United Nations Resolution for an International Day of Peace, which occurs annually on September 21. Several books for youth present the accomplishments of celebrated peace workers, including *Paths to Peace: People Who Changed the World* (Zalben, 2006). In *Seeds of Change* (Johnson, 2010), the growing awareness in Kenyan native Wangari Maathai that "women could do anything they want to, even if it hadn't been done before" preceded her environmental accomplishments in Kenya and her subsequent designation as a Nobel Peace Prize Laureate (p. 17). While stories of recognized activists illustrate the endless possibilities for pursuit of world peace, there is a need for historical accounts of children without fame.

Young people who lived with violence found inner peace in the midst of terrible situations. The power of language helped Ibtisam Barakat cope as a young child during war displacement and separation from her family, then again later when she wrote her memoir in *Tasting the Sky: A Palestinian Childhood* (2007). Peace came to Ibtisam through learning the alphabet and then using it for healing through storytelling. She reflects on coping and healing through language,

> Alef [Arabic alphabet] knows
> That a thread
> Of a story
> Stitches together
> A wound. (Barakat, 2007, p. 171)

The power of language is also evident in *A Song for Cambodia* (Lord, 2008). Relief from the forced labor during a revolution in Cambodia comes from young Arn's ability to play music for the soldiers who occupied his region. His permanent separation first from his family and his nation caused much stress. Playing the Cambodian instrument *khim* was a relief for Arn throughout the difficult transitions. His founding of the organization Children of War during his adulthood gave others peace as well as himself. Relief to others has positive personal effects as well as expressions of caring to those in need. Pilot Halvorsen dropping of candies and gum to people in the midst of war was personally satisfying, during and after his career in the U.S. Air Force. The book *Mercedes and the Chocolate Pilot* (Raven, 2011) shows and explains that during his drops of goodies over Berlin during World War II, "he'd always found in the children's eyes the hope for a better tomorrow" (p. 40). Hope for something better is the typical wish of a child who encounters violence. *One Peace: True Stories of Young Activists* (Wilson, 2008) documents real actions of individual youth stimulated by their hope for life without violence. Their actions demonstrate the desire for harmony in the world as well as in their region, family, and minds. Forgiveness of child soldiers expressed in one poem is crucial for peace and harmony.

> I cannot go any further
> With this shooting and killing that has no border.
> Forgive me now if I injured your brother.
> I was forced to pull the trigger
> By elders who made my childhood wither. (Wilson, 2008, p. 28)

Teaching the her/history of how adults and other youth construed peace increases curriculum relevancy. The nature of human conflicts is similar throughout time. For example, the right to access water has been a global conflict for humans and other life forms (Green Cross, 2013). People continue to experience the same kinds of conflicts in different circumstances. Hence, youth can learn that how people construed peace in the past is quite similar to the types of needs identifiable in their current time. Accounts of how people thought about, wished for, and did something to bring about peace demonstrate a commonality of humanity.

Harmonious Living

Human harmony has been evident when people lived as a whole with each other and their natural world. Dependence on their natural world brought into focus the importance of sustainability. Taking care of earth and the regions of the solar system that humans affect has become forefront again, after disregarding indigenous practices for centuries that were sustainable. The boom of human population and its use of resources for everyone's well-being is a crucial aspect of peace development. Harmony with each other while resources diminish is a task of world leaders, all organizations and individual people. Knowledge about how people in the past lived together harmoniously and managed to not expend or damage natural resources is a learning goal for youth. They need a foundational reference point from the past as well as awareness of goals for the present and future.

Philosophy has offered humans the ideological basis for their lives in harmony with all things (Critchley, 2011). Discernable in literature's presentations are notions of natural harmony, as in balance with nature, as well as human harmony, characterized by agreement of interest in the pursuit of peace. There are philosophical links between feminism and environmentalism evident in their common strives for balance. The issues identified in those approaches to peace exist in other fields that analyze roots of conflict (Plumwood, 1993). A review of projects that environmental heroines maintained reveals the connections of their work in several spheres of human impact (Mok, 2009).

Harmonizing in the pursuit of peace has been crucial for resolving multiple conflicts in a society at the same time. Educated women in the nineteenth century advocated for the need for children's literature and libraries, which paralleled the movement to help immigrant children assimilate through education (Vandergrift, 1996). At that time, child labor was still lawful and many immigrant youth worked without developing skills of literacy. Another example of parallel initiatives was women's activism for female's equal rights and an end to slavery in the United States. Soujourner Truth harmonized the work of abolitionists and suffragettes. While some activists worried that merging causes would diminish the importance of one pursuit for the advancement of another goal, others realized the power in harmonizing efforts.

Role of Youth Literature

In *John Muir, America's First Environmentalist* (Lasky, 2008), the connection between naturalist writing and political action is clear. This Scottish immigrant's observations of and writings about many natural environments documented life forms and places in the United States that most people might have never seen. Those accounts and his political actions resulted with the first national parks and the formation of the Sierra Club, which is an environmental organization with continual political influence. From these corollary efforts of documentation and democracy, people can now visit national parks to observe and sense harmony. The observation of John Muir that people living in cities enjoyed growing plants in tin containers and decorating with cut flowers helped him realize that humans need natural beauty regardless of where they live. The book *A Little Peace* (Kerley, 2007) opens with a hand holding a flower. Its pages continue to show real-life situations around the world where people in different ways create harmony as they spread a little peace. The similarities of how children around the world live depicted in *One World, One Day* (Kerley, 2009) conveys human harmony through cultural similarities. While the distinctness of regions where they live are clear, so are the common types of childhood needs and experiences the book features. In a different turn, *Keeping Corner* (Lasky, 2009), a historical fiction, describes one of the conditions in which childhood experiences are uncommon. It features the historical context of childhood engagement and marriage in India through arranged marriage. The tragedy of adolescent widowhood that Leela experienced required her seclusion and mourning. Individually provided education allows her to learn about the historical responses to social injustice to which people in her region, including Mohandas Gandhi, had been proactively responding. Inspired by these changemakers, Leela takes her first step in that direction as her story ends. The prevention of conflict has harmony as a goal.

Conflict Prevention

Conflict prevention occurs through communication for analysis of existing and anticipated needs. The information about needs occurs through artistic expression, discourse, and even body language. Creativity in meeting needs has been an essential factor in the prevention of harm. While analysis of needs in a situation can occur through multiple genres of literature, presentation of past events is very relevant as conflict education. After they learn from historical literature, youth sometimes ask, *Did that really happen?* They feel a need to verify reality and talk about what happened, including motives and methods in response to conflict. Communication about conflict is a core strategy of programs for youth. They learn the use of *I messages* and other ways of expressing their conflict perceptions. In careful discourse with their peace partners, co-disputants, and proactive peers, they have the goal of conflict description. Proactive peers can describe their own perceptions of a problem, thereby expanding awareness that aids analysis. Multilingual and emerging vocabulary facilitate incorporation of diverse concepts that enhance understanding.

Herstory documents the creation of words for recounting situations in which females had particular needs. The celebrated writer Alice Walker formed the term "womanist" for use in description of women's unequal rights. Her invention of useful language corresponds with the creations by many other women to meet needs they identified. The inventions of women advanced their economic opportunities along with living standards for others as well as themselves. Creations such as the dishwashing machine developed by Josephine Cochrane preserved household goods and improved domestic work, which enabled the pursuit of other activities, including employment (Massachusetts Institute of Technology, 2004). It also reduced family conflict with the decision about whose turn it was to wash dishes.

The herstory of domestic conflict includes giving recognition and ownership of inventions to the male partner of female inventors. The husband of Sybilla Masters in the American colonies received a patent in 1715 by the English courts for her development of cornmeal (Bedi, 2005). The small percentage of women recognized for their creative problem solving reflects the legal, economic, and social constraints they have faced (Library of Congress, 2010). While legal and economic constraints have lessened, social ones remain prevalent, including the lack of female representation in history and science curricula.

The history curriculum underrepresents women and girls as proactive respondents to conflict (Crocco, 2011). What information is available about women and girls as problem preventers predominately promotes white herstory. There is a dearth of information in history and other subject areas about how females of multiple racial and cultural backgrounds advanced peace through their prevention of and response to conflict (Chavez-Garcia, 2013; Dayton & Levenstein, 2012; Miller & Churchryk, 1996). This continual problem undermines the preparation of all youth for conflict prevention, and it sustains a hidden hierarchy of male leadership. In recognition of this imbalance, teachers develop strategies for herstory lessons (Bair, Williams, & Fralinger, 2008; Bix, 2010; Winslow, Crocco, & Berkin, 2009). Although there was designation in the United States of March as Women's History Month, all youth can better understand the strengths that females bring to conflict prevention if they learn diverse herstory year around (Library of Congress, 2013). In that record of herstory, students see how the condition of girls and women in a society affected conflict prevention. Creative Associates International lists strategies for each stage of conflict, with the goal to "Reduce socio-economic sources of conflict" for maintaining the stage of stable peace (2013, para 3). Youth can use this goal for identification of socioeconomic inequities that are the root of a conflict, which literature and life reveal.

Role of Youth Literature

Literature that describes or depicts the imbalances people endured in economic, social, and legal aspects of their lives is useful content in conflict analysis. Asking questions about those situations and comparison with current conditions stimulate the analytical processes needed for discerning conflict sources. The biography of young Louis Armstrong, *If I Only Had a Horn* (Orgill, 1977), shows that although his family and neighbors endured major economic challenges, they nevertheless contributed the coins they had to fund music education for children. Like young Louis Armstrong, Josephine Baker endured poverty as a child and dreamed of a career in performance. The book *Ragtime Tumpie* (Schroeder, 1989) beautifully illustrates how that childhood dream sustained Josephine Baker all the way to international fame as a dancer and mother of the "Rainbow Tribe," which was her family of adopted children. At this time when performing arts have a back-row seat in childhood education, these biographies illustrate how performance skills prevented lifelong poverty for African Americans enduring structural conflicts throughout their lives. The creator of cartoons, Mickey Mouse and Disneyland, Walter Elias Disney, remembered the discipline he endured as a child for painting animals on his family's farmhouse. The book *Akira to Zoltán: Twenty-Six Men Who Changed the World* provides this quote of Disney: "I think it's important to have a good hard failure when you're young" (Chin-Lee, 2006, p. 26). Another illustration of this phenomenon in this same book is the short biography of Akira Kurosawa who failed the entrance exam to art school but went on to become a highly awarded director of movies that featured peace themes (Chin-Lee, 2006). Chin-Lee's quote of Xavier Cugat Mingall, a Latino musician, further emphasizes the importance of inner peace through pursuit of one's desire, "I would rather play 'Chiquita Banana' and have my swimming pool than play Bach and starve" (2006, p. 27). Avoiding inner conflict by making a livelihood out of the activity one enjoys prevents dissatisfaction. The book *S'elavie, That is Life: A Haitian Story of Hope* (Landowne, 2004) illustrates collective action of homeless children, not only for their survival, but also for raising awareness. The Haitian children managed not only to paint murals on their shelter they constructed but also made radio shows with their stories and songs. These efforts prevented life-threatening conditions on the city streets and helped others understand the contributions homeless youth can make in a society. Historical fiction that describes real conditions and events is another source for learning her/history. An analytical use of such fiction with students involves the following steps.

1. Provide students historical information: maps, advertisements, and literature.
2. Teach about the genre and production of historical fiction.
3. Support student reading of the historical fiction.
4. Facilitate student analysis of the content through historical investigation
5. Stimulate student reflection on the value of that fiction when it deviates from history.

(Adapted from Schwebel, 2011).

The conflicts historical fiction presents are also useful for identification of similar contemporary situations that need attention. The process of enmity, that causes perception of an enemy, is evident in historical literature. Identification of the techniques that render enmity enables detection of them in literature and propaganda (Keen, 1986). With skill in analysis of conflict, youth can focus on harm-free responses to it as well as its prevention (Spiegel, 2010).

Avoidance and Repair of Harm

Peace her/history informs about people and methods that avoided violence as a problem response. It also documents repair of damages made in conflict. These accounts are valuable for multiple purposes in social education, as well as literacy. First, they provide a record of human capabilities throughout time for not using harm. Second, they demonstrate the relevance and use of peace as a goal for responding to conflict. Third, they can inspire youth for work towards that goal in their own lives. Fourth, they build hope for accomplishing peace. Such hope can sustain life where there is despair from experience with direct violence. Fifth, they provide strategies for consideration in current and future responses to conflict. Additionally, they indicate a direction for inquiry and models for historical research.

Analyses of peace education in the United States identified the continual efforts throughout centuries. Pursuit of peace in families, cultural groups, institutions besides schools and faith centers, as well as political movements, provide situations for learning (Howlett & Harris, 2010; Stomfay-Stitz, 1993). In her analysis of interactions that became *Cultures of Peace*, Boulding (2000) identified many sites in communities where learning for peace occurred. Much of the education was informal instruction about avoidance of harm while dealing with conflict. Formal lessons that incorporated peace components typically incorporated communication about issues humans faced. Student and parent writing in response journals enabled their communication about presentations in literature. The activity allowed parent demonstration of dispositions that support peace, including, " (a) empathy, (b) a positive outlook on life, (c) an understanding of both sides of the issue, (d) a statement of justification and/or (e) questions to encourage their children to contemplate further" (Farris, Howe, & Fuhler, 1998, p. 3). It is an opportunity for family interpretation of history with their particular insights and analytical approaches. A family whose ancestors directly experienced an historical event may have oral accounts passed on to them or recent experience with an ongoing conflict like cultural discrimination. They likely have particular ways of thinking about events, influenced by their cultural norms. Perhaps they adhere to *ahimsa*, translated from Sanskrit as do not harm, that is a virtue in philosophical and spiritual traditions of India. That adherence in a world filled with violence comes from purposeful living.

Purposefully learning the her/history of peace is different from conventional presentations in social studies. It features notions and records of avoiding harm and pursing restoration after damage. This approach departs from the predominance of violence as a necessary response to political, cultural, and other types of conflict.

History has a role in formation of individual, social, and political identities. It also passes on cultural codes for thought and action. When it legitimates the use of military for response to conflict, it conveys a culture of violence. Part of that culture is evident in promotion of military involvement as an expression of masculinity (Noddings, 2012). When it forefronts the achievements of people with commitments to not harm during political activities, it demonstrates other possibilities for change. Knowledge about the choice if using violent or nonviolent responses to political conflict has been helpful for overcoming fatalism of youth. When they encounter social and political issues and the requirement to identify optimal responses to them, they do more than justify their decisions. They clarify their awareness, values, and opportunities for making change. David Hostetter (2009) reflects that "oral history interviews have proved to be an important window into the personal histories of students as well a strong link to local history" (p, 507). We have found this to be evident in the community research our own students conduct. They develop insights and dispositions that support repair of harm. Historical empathy is an example of a disposition developed in the study of peace (Alpargu, Sahin, & Yazici, (2009). The role of empathy in peace education is central. The continual failure of conventional history in cultivation of empathy underscores the importance of cultivating caring through use of literature. Literature that presents to youth true accounts of careful reduction and repair of harm is crucial curriculum.

Role of Youth Literature

Stories about caring exist worldwide. Here, we mention a few as a sampling of what is available for use as curriculum. A Euro-American's adoption of indigenous Carlos Montezuma, after destruction of Carlos's Yavapai village by the Army in the southwestern United States represents an act of caring. *A Boy Named Beckoning* (Capaldi, 2008) is a biographic presentation of Montezuma's childhood experiences. The caring experiences of his childhood supported his education and professional accomplishments as a physician and activist for the rights of indigenous peoples, including citizenship in the United States. The book identifies the Indian Citizenship Act of 1924 that passed after Dr. Montezuma's speech to the US Senate in 1916. In *Wangari's Trees of Peace* (Winter, 2008), the preservation of deforested land by women of Kenya features not only repair of their ecosystem but also shows how that work generated necessary income for them as well as closer firewood that they needed. The defiant stance Wangari took for allowing planting by women, versus only men, was an act of bravery that landed her in jail. Bravery is not the main theme of book *Gandhi* (Demi, 2001). Yet, it is very evident as a disposition that sustained the many courageous acts Gandhi made in South Africa and India for social and political peace.

Commitment to non-harm in the pursuit of rights and a conviction to care for everyone demonstrates the importance of determination. The biography *Jane Addams, Champion of Democracy* (Fradin & Fradin, 2006) contains many photographs of situations that needed improvement. Jane Addams's expanding commitments to transformation of corruption in Chicago and the care of its impoverished people is clear in this comprehensive, yet readable, book. It also presents her other pursuits in social reform, ending lynching of African Americans. The book *Civic Passions: Seven Who Launched Progressive America and What They Teach Us* (Tichi, 2009) presents the repair work of Addams's contemporaries. While the reading level of the book is very advanced, its pictures are useful for lessons about harmful conditions in America and people who worked hard to change them. Its chapters feature female activism by Alice Hamilton, M.D., Julia Lathrop, Florence Kelley, and Ida B. Wells-Barnett, along with the accomplishments of male reformers in the same era: John Commons, Luis D. Brandeis, and Walter Rauschenbusch. With a need for information about the work of diverse females, Adrea Pinkney's (2000) book *Let It Shine, Stories of Black Women Freedom Fighters* addresses that need. She provides ten easily read and beautifully illustrated biographies of female change-makers. Each chapter provides a quote that gives insights to the experiences of these formidable females in US herstory. For example, the quote of Rosa Parks addresses a need in children's literature. Her statement, "The only tired I was, was tired of giving in," clarifies one reason Rosa became involved in the civil rights movement and her early integration of the Montgomery, Alabama chapter of the National Association for the Advancement of Colored People. The lack of information in much literature for youth about Rosa's activities prior to the bus incident that brought her fame demonstrates the narrow presentation of herstory. The complexities of motivations, strategies, and their outcomes that women and girls experienced are useful information. Youth can not only understand that females had strong roles in shaping the nation as well as their families but also the ways women and girls facilitated change are worthy of consideration.

With awareness of the active role females had in responding to structural conflicts, it is easier to understand the importance of everyone's involvement in preventing and repairing harm. Having male and female models in history that accomplished caring for others and the environment are crucial motivators. Youth can see that recognizing needs in society as well as personal necessities has evidently been gratifying for the change agents as well as helpful to others.

Fulfillment of Needs

Peace her/history describes the activities that people did to meet an evident need. Each story presents an account of what happened. It may recount not only the actions but also interpret the perceptions of needs that stimulated the response to them. The interpretation of the behaviors and perceptions of a person or group who took action usually presents one viewpoint. For example, interpretation may be of a disruptor who caused conflicts or of a heroine who advanced well-being. Analysis of each interpretation reveals whose needs the her/history represents. Youth must develop such analysis skills with historical accounts so they can realize what other information needs inclusion in understanding a conflict situation. With awareness of missing information, they understand why there is a need for finding out more about what happened. Equipped with multiple accounts of an event enables reflection on the effects each account has. People can identify inner feelings that occur when reading one historical version versus another. The feelings indicate effects of the literature, including attitudes towards those described in the history and the author who produced that account.

Analyses of history and curriculum that includes it for social education identified discernable goals. One is legitimation of the state or nation, including its political, economic, and social activities. Pedagogical questions arise. How does the history of a war justify violence? What interest and needs of each nation involved in the event does the historical account include (Langager, 2009; Zajada & Zajada, 2002)? Related to the legitimation need is the preservation of a nation through cultivation of identity as its citizen and patriotism (Bass, 2005; Setalvad, 2010). The goal is advancing feelings of respect for one's nation. Another need that historical accounts accomplish is passing on of national culture. Normalization of beliefs and practices in a nation occurs through stories that associate those norms with success. Featuring the accomplishments of a nation by particular means and populations in it renders those activities as the national norm. Recounting the military's experiences in national history preserves the belief that preparation for violence is normal and needed for national well-being. In this vein, consider the effect of focusing instead on diplomacy and other methods that avoided harm by a nation. Advancing patriarchy, male dominance, through a gender imbalance is another illustration of cultural maintenance. Portraying one group as dependent on another obscures the power and needs of the dominated group, including equal rights. The distraction of who did what for whom that imbalanced history renders is a clue to unmet needs. One group does not need the aid of another unless there is a power imbalance. The term "hegemony of peace" that Weiner (2005) uses refers to power imbalance during times that history characterizes as peaceful. There is no peace when the needs of an individual or group are unfulfilled because of disempowerment by another. The dominance of history over herstory, and other male-orientations in education, demonstrate this hegemony.

There are several reasons that herstory needs equality as learning content for youth. A clear one is representation balance. Opportunities for developing different ways of seeing and responding to conflict are other needs for youth learning of inclusive her/history. Inclusion means not only balancing gendered production of history and genders as topic within it (Riley, 2007) but also an essential process of need fulfillment for conflict management (Papagianni, 2009). There are educational benefits of including diverse accounts about multiple cultures involved in events (Moffett, 2002). Part of that diversity must also be representation of youth in different cultures as active participants in affecting change. The dearth of girls represented as active and effective conflict managers, initiators of change, and leaders perpetuates male dominance. One more reason to have inclusive of her/history is a demonstration that change-makers were not exceptional people (Saeidi, 2012). Youth need to see how typical people in different times and locations decided to meet a need. There should be a demonstration to youth that fulfillment of a need in society is not limited to one gender or cultural group (Rosenberg, 1990).

Use of literature for social education is a widespread practice. Facilitation of literacy instruction in social education is another way that curriculum integration happens (Paquette & Kaufman, 2008). Integration of arts with these two subject areas enhances the learning of youth through expressions of perceptions and understandings they have while interacting with literature and each other. Providing a "social curriculum" involves the collaboration of youth as they co-construct the meaning of historical literature (MacPhee & Whitecotton, 2011). Carefully selected literature enabling their understanding of needs, which avoids misconceptions about populationsthat some literature about indigenous peoples contains (Meyer, 2011). Due to a lack of literature geared toward youth that features Native Americans, literature for adults can be read and used to tell stories or develop needed curriculum. For example, the autobiography of Wilma Mankiller (Mankiller & Wallis, 1993), activist and first female chief of the Cherokee Nation, serves this purpose.

Role of Youth Literature

Finding sufficient literature about diverse peoples who fulfilled needs requires use of Internet resources due to a lack of books. Although printed books for youth contain a few stories about the helpful accomplishments of indigenous and other dominated groups, literature online fills the current gap. The contents provided by the Women's History Project (2014) online is one resource. Currently, it has a webpage titled "When Native American Women First Met Europeans" with brief accounts of many indigenous females who were helpful to Europeans (Zierdt, 2009) The Women's History Project also sells literature and curriculum that support herstory. Their product *Rachel, The Story of Rachel Carson* (Ehrlich, 2003) features a biography starting with childhood experiences that influenced her work as an environmentalist. Her most famous book, *Silent Spring*, brought national attention to the widespread harm of pesticide use. Speaking out about harm is always needed and requires courage when that act is a threat to the well-being of the alarmist. Hence, accounts of people who took those risks demonstrate the importance of courage for need fulfillment. The importance of courage is very evident in the biography *Ida B. Wells, Let the Truth Be Told* (2008). The book jacket explains, "An activist, educator, writer, journalist, suffragette and pioneering voice against the horror of lynching, she used fierce determination and the power of the pen to educate the world" (Meyers, 2008). Communicating in a national administration about the need to use nonharmful responses to violence is a need that the first US congresswoman addressed. She had already become accustomed to pointing out political problems when she advocated prior to women's rights throughout the nation for their voting opportunities. The book *Jeannette Rankin, Political Pioneer* (Woelfe, 2007) describes and provides many photos of her work for rights, justice, and peace. "At age eighty-seven she marched in Washington, D.C., at the head of the Jeannette Ranking Peace Parade, made up of five thousand women" (Woelfe, book jacket).

While speaking out is important, facilitating escapes from slavery on the underground railroad was an incredible act of courage by not only African American conductors like Harriet

Tubman and William Sill; youth should also read accounts about the bravery of American Quakers such as Levi Coffin. One picture book that offers an illustration of song use by conductors is *Follow the Drinking Gourd* (Winter, 2008). This story and others that demonstrate the importance of teamwork in the pursuit of peace are valuable lessons for youth. Another book by Jeanette Winter, whose literature is so engaging, features teamwork in protection of library books during the wartime bombing of Iraq. *The Librarian of Basra* (Winter, 2004) recounts the timely initiatives of Alia Muhammad Baker during the Gulf War, which saved the books she moved out of the library before destruction of the library by bombs. Her creativity in the initiative is an essential aspect of peace work. The father of modern peace education, Johan Galtung (2004), points out the crucial need for creativity in solving problems.

The available her/history of inventions evidences the role of human creativity in problem solving. People can create solutions. While the record of female innovation is less evident in school curriculum, there is a need to incorporate literature about their accomplishments. In the book *American Women Inventors* (Camp, 2004) readers learn how astronaut and inventor Ellen Ochoa responded to the conflict of being away from her young child during her space missions. She made a video that her husband played for their child on the nights she was away. The accounts of how females juggled domestic responsibilities and work outside of the home makes a needed demonstration in a world where women are still offered less professional opportunities and less pay than men in the same positions. Addressing the needs of people in poverty, after one has left it due to professional success, demonstrates commitment as well as caring. In *Women Inventors Who Changed the World* (Braun, 2012), the biography of Patricia Bath features this path. She returned to her home of Harlem after becoming an eye doctor and instituted a community health program for the many blind residents there. Her invention of laser surgery for the removal of cataracts had a worldwide effect on the reduction of blindness. The first Hispanic to be US Surgeon General was Puerto Rican Antonia Novello. In the book *Ladies First, 40 Daring American Women Who Were Second to None* (Allison, 2006), Novello reflects that " I want to be able to look back someday and say 'I did make a difference.' Whether it was to open the minds of people to think that a woman can do a good job, or whether it's the fact that so many kids out there think that they could be me" (p. 140). The biography of Maria Tallchief, first Native American prima ballerina, illustrates one of several challenges in being the first representative of one's group. "Because it was unusual to see a Native American in ballet, I had to fight not to be exploited. I wanted to be recognized for my dancing and not solely because I was Osage" (Allison, 2006, p. 172). Work in the arts has been a beneficial profession and as well as a means of expression for those who endured oppression. Demonstrating the artistic talent that dominated, indeed enslaved, people exhibit is the book *Dave, the Potter, Artist, Poet, Slave* (Hill, 2010). The creative works Dave managed to produce in pottery and poetry that responded to his own intrapersonal needs, as well as that of people now who analyze slaves' responses to injustice.

Development of empathy for those who face systemic conflict, life-threatening situations, and other problems is one goal. Another is praxis, or purposeful action, by youth that responds to needs they discern in literature. Stories that feature praxis by youth can inspire response to current needs. Families, teachers, and others who share literature with youth can select books that demonstrate praxis. One example of this is *Give a Goat* (Schrock, 2008). It features projects by children involving fundraising for relief organizations including Heifer International and Red Cross. Providing relief is an empathetic response to conditions that evidence unfair treatment. Youth can do more than provide relief; they can participate in activism that addresses injustice and other forms of societal conflict.

Social and Legal Justice

The history of rights infringements brings to light social and legal justice. Education about injustice in social and legal realms has an important role in peace education. It brings awareness of imbalance that is the seed of conflict. Youth typically understand imbalance conflict when one has more of something than another or nothing. Stories that feature imbalance are relevant to those situations in real life. Information and discussion about what and who has social and legal rights sensitizes students to the importance of justice in many different contexts. Current events as well as history described in literature for youth raises their awareness about situations where rights needed balancing. It also provides information about how people have worked for resolution of injustice conflicts.

True stories about how people proactively responded to injustice demonstrate the importance of noncomplacency with that situation. The record of government response to those actions provides political situations for analysis. For example, the banning in Ecuador of the Pachamama Alliance (2014), which has rights advocates in the Amazon, is a conflict that calls for student analysis of peoples' actions. Youth can consider the economic interests of government and the rights of life forms in an area that economic advancement impacts. Those considerations will feature perspectives of different populations and life forms. The revelations in those perspectives enable cultivation of pluralism, which is the idea of inclusive belonging as part of a place and time. Theories of social and legal justice clarify the frameworks people have used for those considerations.

Theories evident in education about social and legal justice clarify the role of politics and identity. The idea of distributive justice (Rawls, 1971) facilitates examination of material distribution for imbalance. The roots of injustice grow from exploitation that prevents actualization of people.

Exploitation of laborers for the economic advantage of consumers is one example. Another is harm to the biosphere that sustains an indigenous population surviving with the natural resources in their region. The dualism of redistribution and recognition as a population is another theory incorporated in the analyses of injustice (Fraser, 2003). This theory helps explain how exclusion of identity and culture cause imbalance that impedes fair redistribution of resources.

Education about social and legal justice as her/history demonstrates the goal of understanding and improving life conditions for different populations (Grant & Gibson, 2013). It is limitless to include all life forms as well as cultural groups. Literature about people who strove for justice can provide the knowledge foundation for youth who will face such challenges throughout their lives.

Role of Youth Literature

There are numerous accounts of people who responded to systemic conflict and violence in ways that avoided physical harm. For each person who had widespread results in that type of response there are multiple sources of literature. The few examples mentioned here describe what is useful with youth. The biography on Mohandas Gandhi (Martin, 2001) features several photographs throughout his life with a timeline. Additionally, it has a glossary as an aid to comprehension of several terms, including *ahimisa*, the Hindu principal of nonviolence, and *satyagraha*, insistence on truth. Although the history of Gandhi presents him as a nonviolence mentor for responses to injustice by Martin Luther King Jr. and Nelson Mandela, he had a predecessor in the United States. The Krass (1988) biography of Sojourner Truth provides several photos and illustrations that contextualize her life. It describes her accomplishments as a nonviolent activist along with her record as a former slave who advanced abolition and then voting rights for all citizens. The book *With Courage and Cloth: Winning the Fight for a Woman's Right to Vote* (Bausum, 2004) features photos of female activists and their daughters in protests. The photographic presentation on every page in *Children of the Civil Rights Era* (Welch, 2001) is a very useful source for learning about the role of youth in change efforts. The illustrations and activities in the book make difficult issues and concepts comprehensible to youth. Activities from *Learning About Nonviolence*, including John Lewis's Nashville Code for protestors, "Don't strike back or curse if abused" (p. 40) provide strategies for youth to practice. *Freedom Walkers, The Story of the Montgomery Bus Boycott* (Freedman, 2006) depicts that code in action with illustrations of no reciprocal harm by youth being attacked with a police dog. The question activist Fannie Lou Hamer asked after she was beaten and shot for her protesting was, "Is this America?" (Adler, 2007). The title *Heroes for Civil Rights* by Adler is apt given the violence endured during work to eliminate injustices.

Instruction about social and legal justice has occurred in all subject areas that schools include. Literature is a good resource for each of those contexts. Instruction in language arts and reading literature that features accounts of justice work and current situations where there is a need for justice can connect to lessons in other subject areas on the same historical time period. Use of different accounts for broadening perspectives of what happened enhances awareness of injustice. The Peacebuttons (2014) website provides a brief description for each day of the year about peace and social justice efforts.

Questions to Consider for Peace Her/History through Youth Literature

From Evaluation Criteria for Youth Literature in Peace Education

Copyright Candice C. Carter and Shelly Clay-Robison

1. Were multiple sources of information used to incorporate diverse perspectives?

2. Does the information represent more than the dominant members of the society?
3. Is the information gender-inclusive, showing involvement by females and males?
4. Was the involvement of children described?
5. Does the information address cultural diversity?
6. Are value differences of the described populations presented?
7. Are the multiple roots of the presented conflicts included?

Summary

Peace history is an interpretation of human interactions while they responded to conflict. It describes thoughts and change efforts. Herstory includes females as researchers and subjects. Inclusive peace her/history features multiple meanings through incorporation of diverse perspectives of a situation. With multiple accounts of an occurrence, youth understand why there is a need for more than one description of a situation. Crucial for peace work is an understanding of different needs in a situation. Her/history provides youth with practice in conflict analysis as well as their identification of interpretation techniques. Youth study of peace her/history balances the canon of literature provided in schools that emphasizes violence as a response to conflict. Facilitation of that learning can happen across subject areas in school. The dearth of print literature for youth about peace her/history demonstrates the need to use other sources for needed instruction. Oral accounts from people youth can interview, song lyrics, and visual arts as well as resources on the Internet are worthwhile learning supplements. There is a need for youth as well as adult development of literature for peace her/history.

8

Developmental Learning

Educating for peace is not a simple matter of teaching facts and skills. Learning to live peacefully is a lifelong, developmental, and dynamic process. Foundations of peaceful living are much the same throughout life, but perceptions of self, others, and the world are understood differently according to age, development, and experience (Harris & Morrison, 2013). It is important, therefore, to consider children's cognitive, social, and emotional development, along with their cultures, experiences, and needs when teaching concepts and choosing books about peace (Piaget, 1971; Vygotsky, 1978; Wheeler, 2004).

Approaching peace education with a developmental perspective allows for responding to individual characteristics, needs, and experiences. Inclusive literature can support positive views of self and others, appreciation for diversity, and understanding social contexts (Emery, 2002; Mendoza & Rees, 2001). At the same time, literature offers characters and scenarios to consider as a venue for developing social skills needed for cooperation and conflict transformation.

Fully integrating literature that reflects issues related to peaceful living helps children develop essential dispositions and skills (Lantieri & Patti, 1996). Literature that affirms identity promotes healthy self-concepts and confidence for interacting positively with others. Reading and discussing literature that portrays diversity addresses children's natural curiosity about differences while fostering mutual respect and understanding (Ching, 2005; Derman-Sparks & Edwards, 2010). Realistic portrayals of diverse characters illustrate common humanity and allow youth to make personal connections and care about others who may be in some ways different from themselves (Beaty, 1996). Sharing ideas and engaging in dialogue about inclusive literature is a forum to develop habits of thinking with and about multiple perspectives (Dewey, 1938). An inclusive approach allows children, at every level, relate to a range of people, perceptions, and contexts that provide a foundation for caring and positive interactions.

Making personal connections and caring about others creates a foundation for harmonious relationships (Noddings, 2008). Self-awareness, understanding of others, and positive socials skills are needed to develop and maintain goodwill. A variety of youth literature addresses feelings, needs, and skills for developing mutual understanding, cooperation, and problem solving.

Successful prevention and transformation of conflict is supported by self-awareness, caring for others, abilities to consider multiple perspectives, and a willingness to seek mutually beneficial solutions (Galtung, 2004; Rosenberg, 2003a). Caring about and respecting others serve as necessary precursors to thinking critically about conflicts that may challenge deeply held and previously unexamined beliefs (Rosenberg, 2005b). Inclusive literature that addresses concepts of peace can be used at different levels of complexity to support children's development of critical thinking about personal relationships, diversity, and social change (Ching, 2005; Levin 2007). Youth literature can be used to present increasingly complex and controversial issues in ways that allow children to consider different perspectives and apply skills according to their development and needs (Picower, 2012).

Opportunities for all to meet basic needs are essential for lasting peace. Sharing literature that illustrates the common humanity and contributions of a wide range of individuals and groups is important because historically, curriculum has underrepresented the contributions, experiences, and voices of dominated groups (Banks, 1999; Darder, 2012). Awareness of previously unrecognized contributions increases mutual respect and challenges biased notions that some groups are more or less worthy than others. Literature can support youth in understanding interdependence, diverse approaches to meeting needs, and sources of inequity.

Youth literature can be a source of knowledge that leads to peaceful action to address social problems. Recognizing and caring about human rights and injustice are requisite to working for change (Adams, Bell, & Griffin, 2007). Equally important is developing orientations and skills for achieving change through harm-free action (Rosenberg, 2005b). Literature can inspire and inform youth with stories of action by individuals and groups to promote peace and justice. At the same time, stories illustrate the commitment and sacrifices that often accompany such action. Inspiring literature along with guidance from thoughtful, caring adults enables youth to conceptualize and engage in peaceful social action.

Construal of Peace

Perceptions of the world that contribute to peaceful living begin during the first years of life. From birth, humans are drawn to social relationships and their very survival depends on others (Derman-Sparks & Edwards, 2010). When their needs are regularly met through caring interactions, babies develop trust and sense of the world as a safe and secure place. Those experiences are seeds for sprouting belief in peace as a possibility. In a nurturing environment, children and older youth experience love and compassion. Those positive experiences are fertilizer for cultivation of healthy identities and the ability to bond with others.

Literature can reinforce loving relationships and positive self-concepts with soothing language and pleasant images of children and familiar activities. Books depicting familiar themes, with diverse characters build awareness of diversity from the very beginning. For example, *Baby Says*, (Steptoe, 1988), *The I Love You Book* (Parr, 2010), *I Love You Just Because* (Parr, 2006), and *Guess How Much I Love You* (McBratney, 2008) communicate to children that they are important and cherished. *Ten Little Fingers and Ten Little Toes* (Fox, 2008) and *Whose Knees are These (Asim, 2006)* have illustrations and simple language that depict loving adults admiring different babies. *Global Babies* (Global Fund for Children, 2007) uses photographs of infants around the world to depict various approaches to nurturing and care taking. *Baby Learns Colors* (Blacksheep, 2004) portrays a Navajo girl as she grows and learns. Helen Oxenbury offers several books with diverse characters including, *I See* (1995), *I Touch* (1999), and *I Can* (1995) to celebrate the accomplishments and abilities of the very young. Sharing literature with children that affirms their value and depicts loving relationships contributes to development of positive identities and relationships.

Social identities first begin with infants understanding that they are part of a family (Bronfenbrenner, 1979; Derman-Sparks & Edwards, 2010). Children experience a family culture and way of living that contributes to perceptions of who they are and how they fit in the world. The first, intimate environment of home and family may be relatively homogeneous and if that is all they know, children will naturally assume their way of life is the normal, right way of doing things (Copple & Bredekamp, 2009). Appreciation for different ways of living can be fostered with literature that depicts diverse children and families going about daily activities in different ways. Literature that presents diversity, as natural, reinforces positive feelings about their own families and develops understanding of difference that prepares children for diversity outside of the family (Emery, 2002). Themes of home, work, and caretaking are familiar to children and literature that presents different physical appearances, abilities, homes, foods, clothing, and approaches to meeting needs, introduces diversity in a context that relates to children's first experiences. With guidance from adults (Vygotsky, 1978), they are able to understand and respect different types of families along with different ways of being and living.

All Kinds of Children (Simon, 1999), *Families* (Morris, 2000), *Who's in a Family?* (Skutch, 1997), and *All-of-a-Kind Family* (Taylor, 2011) highlight different types of families engaging in activities that are universally recognizable. With these books children can relate to their own experiences and become aware of differences. *You Can Do It* (Dungy, 2010), *Grandfather and I* (Buckley, 1994); *Lola Loves Stories* (McQuinn, 2010), *The Sandwich Swap* (Queen Rania of Jordan, 2010); *My Mum Is a Wonder* (Messaoudi, 2007), *Angel City* (Johnston, 2006), *Mommy, Momma and Me* (Newman, 2009), *Two Many Tamales* (Soto, 1996), *When I Am Old with You* (Johnson, 1990), *Two Pairs of Shoes* (Sanderson, 1998), and *Where Did You Get Your Moccasins* (Wheeler, 1982) are examples of stories written about families from a wide variety of racial, ethnic, religious, and socioeconomic backgrounds. Each tells a good story about family life and loving relationships in a context that affirms cultural identities and informs others.

Perceptions of identity and relationships with others develop throughout life in response to cognitive development, experiences, and expanding social circles. Social messages impact children's personal and social identities, as well as acceptance of difference. Early on, children begin to develop perceptions about socially defined groups, including race and ethnicity, gender, religion, language along with awareness of social class (Connolly, Smith, & Kelly, 2002: Derman-Sparks & Edwards, 2010).

Use of inclusive literature that addresses themes and issues of interest to youth can challenge biased social messages and promote positive self-concepts. Relevant stories facilitate understand and support youth while they navigate increasingly complex interpersonal relationships. For example, *Billy Elliot* (Burgess, 2002) explores gender identity with the story of a young boy's interest in and talent for ballet. *The Evolution of Calpurnia Tate* (Kelly, 2009) explores the relationship of a girl living in a family with six brothers. *The Dream on Blanca's Wall/El Sueno Pegado En La Pared De Blanca: Poems in English and Spanish* (Medina Wordsong, 2004) is a collection of poetry expressing a girl's life with the challenges of poverty and immigration. These books depict diverse situations but address common concerns of youth as they grapple with personal identities within the social world. They present positive portrayals of individual characters that encourage readers to relate at a personal level.

With positive self-concepts and appreciation for difference, children are able to relate to and care about diverse others as people with whom they pursue common goals and mutual well-being.

Harmonious Relationships

Realistic portrayals of diverse characters situated in different social contexts allow children to recognize common humanity, make personal connections, and care about others who are different from themselves. This sort of literature can be a platform for engaging children's questions about difference and fostering prosocial skills needed for harmonious relationships.

Learning skills for living in fellowship with others is supported in groups who have mutual respect and trust because there is an expectation of positive outcomes. Cooperative living skills are particularly difficult for the very young who have limited experiences and difficulty understanding the feelings and perspectives of others (Fields, Perry, & Fields, 2010). Developing the ability to consider the feelings and needs of others begins with self-awareness and development of emotion regulation, or the ability to cope with feelings and control actions related to emotions (Landy, 2002). Literature can help youth of all ages learn that feelings are okay, but that some actions hurt others (Gartrell, 2006). For example, *Mad Isn't Bad: A Child's Book about Anger* (Mundy, 1998) sends the message that there are reasons for anger, everyone is angry at times and provides ideas for responding to anger in ways that help solve the problem without hurting others.

Children need guidance to recognize and express the range of feelings that they experience (Gartrell, 2006; Fields, Perry, & Edwards, 2010; Rosenberg, 2003a). When adults acknowledge those feelings, children learn empathy and begin to understand that other people have feelings, too. An abundance of children's books are available to help children learn to recognize their own and the feelings of others. For example, *The Way I Feel* (Cain, 2000) depicts and names a range of emotions that are familiar to children. *The Feel Good Book* (Parr, 2009) identifies feelings that are enjoyable. *When I Miss You* (Spelman, 2005), addresses the pain children feel when separated from people they love. *Everett Anderson's Goodbye* (Clifton, 1988) explores feelings of grief. Children are encouraged to consider the feelings of other people in *Stand in My Shoes: Kids Learning About Empathy* (Sornson, 2013).

Books for older youth can address feelings and needs in scenarios that relate to their own experiences, yet offer insights into diverse perspectives and situations. James Howe introduces a group of children in *The Misfits* (2003) who are teased for being different in appearance, ability, and sexual orientation. The characters respond, not as victims, but with actions to promote positive change. *Love Ya Bunches* (Myracle, 2009) centers on the friendships and rivalries of a group of girls and offers opportunities to explore the relationship between feelings, needs, and behaviors. *From the Notebooks of Melanin Sun* (Woodson, 2010) portrays, through a boy's journey, a boy's struggle with anger and doubt about his identity and changes in his family. These books address emotions that characterize adolescence through stories of characters that are members of groups that often face bias. Because they are respectfully portrayed, readers can relate on a personal level that fosters caring while offering opportunities for youth to explore their own feelings and actions.

Identifying and understanding feelings is a step toward regulating emotions and reading social cues. With guidance from adults, children can learn prosocial ways to express emotions and empathy for others. Again, children's literature portrays feelings and situations to which children can relate and with guidance, use those examples to identify, then develop, responses that promote harmony. *The Way I Feel* series (Spelman, 2002) helps children to identify and handle a range of emotions including anger, fear, sadness, care, loneliness, jealousy, and happiness. *How to Take the GRRRR Out of Anger* (Verdick, 2002) helps children understand positive ways to express strong feelings. *When I Care about Others* (Spelman, 2002) explores the good feelings that come from caring for others.

Books for older children provide relevant contexts for considering how feelings trigger actions and for reflecting on consequences of different behaviors. *Miracle's Boys* (Woodson, 2006) tells of three orphaned brothers and the different ways they respond to the strong emotions of love, grief, guilt, and anger. *Rain is Not My Indian Name* (Leitich Smith, 2001) is a story of a Native American teen's feelings and responses to her search for identity, grief at losing a friend, and commitment to social justice. These are novels with compelling characters and engaging plots that provide fertile ground for guided discussions about feelings, needs, and actions. *Playground: The Mostly True Story of a Former Bully* (Jackson, 2011) and *Confessions of a Former Bully* (Ludwig, 2012) both present the experiences from the perspective of bullies to reveal some of the feelings and needs that trigger violent behavior. They also discuss the negative consequences and alternatives to violence.

Friendship is a strong motivation to develop empathy and learn to cooperate, so books about friends are particularly effective for developing perspectives, reasoning abilities, and problem-solving abilities. Some books give an overview of ways of thinking and behaving to promote positive relationships. *All My Friends Are Different but We Are All the Same* (Christie, 2012) helps children think about difference and consider others. *We Can Get Along: A Child's Book of Choices* (Rolhling, 1997) conveys that children can make decisions about how to act that affect relationships. *Making Friends* (Rogers, 1996), *The Best Friends Book* (Parr, 1997), and *The Peace Book* (Parr, 2010) show diverse characters working and playing together with images of sharing and cooperation.

All of these books engage children with topics that are important and relevant to them. Guided readings and discussions help children understand the relationship between feelings, actions, and the responses that their actions prompt from others (Steiner, 2008). Discussion and role-play reinforce the messages and help children develop skills to use in real life. When social problems do arise, stories can be reference points to trigger empathy and solve problems collaboratively.

Helping children develop understandings of feelings of self and others, along with abilities to make decisions lays a foundation for lifelong social relationships. As reasoning abilities develop with multiple experiences, youth can build on this foundation to understand and address increasingly complex personal relationships and social issues.

Conflict Prevention

The orientations and skills for harmonious living help to prevent serious conflicts but living together means that inevitably, conflicts will occur between people. Conflicts are a pervasive characteristic of settings with young children and are often viewed by adults as problems to be eliminated (Fields, Perry, & Fields, 2010). While children's conflicts may be difficult and tiring for adults to address, they are essential elements for optimal growth and development. Sonia Nieto

(2006) maintains that acknowledging and working through conflict can lead diverse groups of all ages toward mutual understanding. Conflicts are important events that allow children to develop skills in negotiation and compromise needed for democratic living (Dewey, 1938). In other words, conflicts provide teachable moments when adults can help children advance their psychological, linguistic, and emotional development and achieve positive change (Bronfennbrenner, 1979; Piaget, 1962; Vygotsky, 1978).

The potential benefits of conflict for promoting early (and lifelong) development depend on guidance from caring adults, for children to develop constructive approaches to differing ideas, interests, and actions. Helping children develop respect for self and others, as well as skills for harmonious living, lays a foundation for the skills and dispositions needed for solving problems peacefully (Gomes de Matos, 2008; Rosenberg, 2003b). Constructive approaches to conflict "involve efforts toward mutual problem solving and continuing social interaction" (Wheeler, 2004, p. 10). Conversely, destructive conflict is characterized by threats and attempts to dominate or force compliance without regard to feelings, needs, or the rights of others.

Children's literature can be used to draw upon dispositions toward respect and understandings of others to motivate learning prosocial skills. *Cool Down and Work Through Anger* (Meiners, 2010) addresses the way anger feels and ways to express it without hurting others and provides suggestions for making amends. *Words Are Not for Hurting* (Verdick, 2004) helps children consider words and actions that escalate conflict and cause hard feelings, as well as those that promote mutual understanding and good will. *The Recess Queen* (O'neill, 2002) is the story of Mean Jean, who bullies other children during recess until a new girl asks her to join in play. They become friends and soon the bullying stops. This story allows children to consider the perspectives and needs of characters that lead to conflict.

Children can be introduced to simple strategies for framing interactions with positive language. They can be supported in using "I messages" to communicate feelings and needs and to use language, such as, "thank you, please, excuse me, I'm sorry, or are you okay?" to convey care for others (Fields, Perry, & Fields, 2010; Wheeler, 2004). The following "I Care Rules" can help remind children of strategies for positive communications: (1) We listen to each other, (2) Hands are for helping, not hurting, (3) We use I-Care language, (4) We care about each other's feelings, and (5) We are responsible for what we say and do (Wheeler, 2004, p. 284). Literature can allow children to explore how words and approaches to communication affected characters and situations in stories.

Providing basic vocabulary and skills in positive communication prepares children to apply strategies for conflict resolution. While there are several models (Wichert, 1989; Adams & Wittmer, 2001), the Five Step Approach (Gartrell, 2001) is particularly useful because it is simple enough for children to understand yet, the process can apply at any age. Young children can organize thinking through the conflict by counting the steps on each finger in the following way: (1) Cool down, (2) Identify the problem, (3) Brainstorm, (4) Go for it, and (5) Follow-up. The Five Step Approach not only helps children solve problems but can also be used to analyze conflict situations within text and to prompt suggestions that characters could use to solve their problems.

Talk and Work it Out (Meiners, 2005) provides illustrations and language to demonstrate approaches to conflict resolution that children can apply to their own experiences. The conflict between a brother and sister in *Give It Back!* (Nothman, 2014) could be a forum for children to share their own experiences and help solve a conflict between a brother and sister about sharing their teddy bear. Sam McBratney's *I'm Sorry!* (2006) tells the story of a fight between two friends caused by angry words. The illustrations and text provide opportunities for children to relate to the characters feelings and needs, identify the problem, and brainstorm approaches to transforming the conflict to restore the friendship.

With a foundation of respect and understanding for others children can approach conflict constructively. Literature, with guidance from adults, is a prime venue for developing skills and language to transform conflict and restore inner peace and amicable relations.

Fulfilling Needs

A foundation for peaceful interactions is recognizing the inherent dignity and worth of others (Gomes de Matos, 2008; Rosenberg, 2003a) and literature is a useful tool to counter negative societal messages and deepen mutual understanding and respect (Levin, 2007). Equity of access to the resources necessary for meeting basic needs is a critical aspect for peace. Yet, biased thinking and stereotypes encourage beliefs that some individuals and groups are more worthy than others as a way to explain contrasts of abundance and deprivation.

Literature that depicts the lives of various groups of people disputes stereotypes and promotes respect for the work they do to meet needs and contribute to the well-being families and communities. *Uncle Jed's Barbershop* (Mitchell, 1993) is foremost a story of love, hard work, and generosity. Set in the poverty of the Great Depression and racial oppression it tells the story of how Uncle Jed worked a lifetime to fulfill his dream, to own his own, shop at the age of 79. *Castle on Viola Street* (DiSalvo, 2001) tells the story of a family who, through good fortune and hard work, is able to move from their rundown apartment into a home that is being renovated by the city. *Those Shoes* (Boelts, 2009) shares the experience of a young boy who is unable to have shoes that he desperately wants, so that he can fit in at school, because his family only has enough "for needs, not wants." *One Potato, Two Potato* (DeFelice, 2006), *Spuds* (Hesse, 2008), *Lucky Beans* (Birtha, 2010), and *The Secret River* (Rawlings, 2011) are stories of families who struggle to meet their needs with ingenuity and hope for a better future. These stories provide windows into the lives of compelling characters whose lives are lived differently, yet illustrate positive qualities to which all readers can relate.

Through personal experiences, observing others, and through the media, children become aware of the social standing of their home culture within society. Over time, youth become vulnerable to internalized "oppression" or "privilege" (Derman-Sparks & Edwards, 2010). Internalized oppression refers to negative beliefs about one's identity as inferior, while internalized privilege refers to beliefs of superiority and entitlement. Literature that depicts diverse conditions and ways of meeting needs in a positive light supports children's development of realistic concepts about self and others (Ching, 2005). At the same time, literature that addresses difficult topics, such as poverty or discrimination and exploitation can help youth begin to understand the causes of inequity.

Side by side/Lado a lado: The story of Dolores Huerta and Cesar Chavez/ La historia de Dolores Huerta y Cesar Chaves (Brown, 2010) portrays the poverty and hardships that face migrant farm workers who work to create better lives for their families. The families are portrayed with dignity and honor. At the same time, it is clear that although the nation depends upon their labor to harvest and provide food, they receive little reward for brutal work and live in poverty.

Children also form ideas about who is important by observing who is and isn't visible in books, media, and observed positions of authority (Derman-Sparks & Edwards, 2010). Literature that highlights the work and achievements of members of the underrepresented reinforces the notion that everyone is important and that people from every conceivable group have made significant and wide-ranging contributions to the world. Issues of social justice become apparent and contextualized in telling the stories of real people whose lives were impacted by injustice.

For example, *Tomas and the Library Lady* (Mora, 2000) is the story of Tomas Rivera, who began life in a family of migrant farm workers and became a Chancellor in the University of California system. His story emphasizes warm family relationships and joy alongside the harsh conditions of migrant life. It also illustrates the family support that enabled him to overcome obstacles to success. *When Marian Sang: The True Recital of Marian Anderson* (Munoz Ryan, 2002) is the story of Marian Anderson's journey to become one of the world's most acclaimed opera singers. Although she was an American, she began her career in Europe, because discrimination against African Americans prevented her from studying or performing professionally in the United States. She became an international success and eventually returned to the United States to perform. Her performance at the Lincoln Memorial in 1939 was historic with a racially integrated audience of 75,000 people. *My Heroes, My People: African Americans and Native Americans in the West* (Monceaux & Katcher, 1999) is a collection of biographies and portraits telling stories about historical figures in the history of the United States. *Benjamin Banneker: Pioneering Scientist* (Wadsworth, 2003) is a biography of the son of a former slave and indentured servant during the 1800s. His many accomplishments included developing the first fully functioning clock in America. *Code Talker: A Novel about the Navajo Marines of World War Two* (Bruchac, 2006) illustrates Navajo culture, spirituality, and honor in telling the experiences of Navajo soldiers as "code-talkers" during the war. Although their language was forbidden to them as students in Indian boarding schools, it was highly valued when they were soldiers for secret communications whose code could not be broken. The story also highlights the sacrifices and service of Native Americans.

Using literature to build awareness of the important roles played by diverse groups fosters appreciation and respect, while stimulating questions and opportunities for thinking critically about unequal access to resources and power.

Social and Legal Justice

For young children, justice is best understood as fairness (Piaget, 1966). In groups, they are conscious of whether access to toys, tools, space, food, and attention from adults is equitable. They are painfully conscious of the effects of being left out and know the importance of belonging. While they are aware of their own desires and feelings, they may not recognize the needs and feelings of others. With help, they begin to understand that fairness also applies to others and requires cooperation and sometimes, deferring their own desires.

Once again, understanding and respect are needed to create conditions of caring for the needs and rights of others. Literature exposes children to multiple perspectives and situations that allow them to empathize with characters who are not treated fairly or whose needs are not being met. *The Sandbox* (Archibold, 2007) presents a dilemma when two children refuse to allow another child to join in the play and offers opportunities for children to develop solutions that would be fair to everyone. Many other books present situations that are familiar to children. For example, *I Won't Share* (Wilhelm, 2010) is a story that will resonate with children as it tells the experiences of Noodle, the dog, who has no one to play with because he won't share with his friends. Other experiences that will be familiar are presented in *It's My Turn* (Bedford, 2001), a story of playground fun that ends when friends don't take turns. *The Doorbell Rang* (Hutchins, 1989) presents the problem of how to equally share cookies and *Everett Anderson's Friend* (Clifton, 1999) promotes opportunities for critical thinking about gender and bias, when Everett becomes friends with his new neighbor after his initial disappointment that she is a girl.

Stories can also help young children become aware of the possibilities for creating positive change through personal actions. *Yertle the Turtle* (Seuss, 2013) shows all of the turtles being exploited by King Yertle. A lowly worker, Mack demonstrates the power to create change by standing up for everyone's rights. These stories plant seeds of empowerment.

Ideas for taking positive action can be nurtured with true stories of real children who have taken action to make the world a better place. Engaging youth literature can stimulate thinking about concepts of fairness and ways to behave that are fair to one's self and others. Learning about fairness through literature that relates to personal experiences with peers creates a cognitive framework to enable them to consider larger contexts and begin to recognize needs for living, such as, food, water, and shelter.

Because children's experiences are limited, those who live in relatively comfortable conditions are often unaware that some people live in want. Children's literature can expose them to conditions beyond their own experiences. Through stories of compelling characters about which they care, they can develop empathy and explore causes of injustice.

Literature can help children become aware of social issues and inspire action for change. For example, *Real Kids, Real Stories, Real Change: Courageous Actions Around the World* (Sundem, 2010) tell stories through words and photographs of children who have used their skills and abilities to make positive contributions to a world in need. Youth can especially relate to books about historical and current conditions of child labor because the workers represent their own peer groups.

Susan Campbell Bartoletti (1999) uses photographs and stories of workers in *Growing Up in Coal Country* to illustrate what childhood was like working long hours in dangerous coal mines during the early 1900s. *Counting on Grace* (Winthrop, 2007) tells the story of a 12-year-old girl who worked in a factory to pay family debts. Russell Freedman (1998) uses Lewis Hines historic photographs in *Kids at Work: Lewis Hine and the Crusade Against Child Labor* to provide an in-depth look at the lives and conditions of child laborers during the period between 1908 and 1918. The images and descriptions of children, who were as young as three years of age, portray the loss of childhood and the suffering that was caused by exploiting children for cheap labor. Lewis's work raised public consciousness and contributed to the enactment of laws to protect children in the United States.

Child Labor Today: A Human Rights Issue (Herumin, 2007) presents historical and contemporary conditions of children, throughout the world, who are forced to work in brutal conditions. At the age of 12, Craig Kielburger learned of the existence of child labor and traveled to talk with and learn from child laborers in South Asia. In *Free the Children* (Kielburger, 2010), he shares what he learned about the abusive living and working conditions of children throughout the developing world and implores people everywhere to join in efforts to create change.

Fire at the Triangle Factory (Littlefield, 1995) is a story of friendship between two girls working at the factory. Their story highlights the unsafe and exploitive labor practices that led to the infamous factory fire. *Brave Girl, Clara and the Shirtwaist Maker's Strike of 1909* (Markel, 2013) tells of a young Ukrainian immigrant who led a strike for humane working conditions in the factory where she worked. These stories encourage empowerment with positive action that can lead to positive changes.

When children become aware of unmet needs and begin to understand the causes, there is hope that they will choose to live in a way that promotes change. Literature can help build awareness of both causes of inequity and provide examples of actions that helped to make a difference.

Questions to Consider for Developmental Learning with Youth Literature

From Evaluation Criteria for Youth Literature in Peace Education

Copyright Candice C. Carter and Shelly Clay-Robison

1. Is the literature age appropriate?
2. Is the literature cognitively appropriate?
3. Is the literature therapeutically appropriate for particular needs?

4. Does the literature stimulate reader's questions?
5. Does the literature invite critical thinking?
6. Does the literature provide sufficiently complex strategies?
7. Are recommended skills easy to identify?
8. Is the literature highly engaging?
9. Does the literature effectively demonstrate peace strategies?
10. Are peace skills obvious and easily implemented in the literature?

Summary

Foundations of care and understanding, along with skills for peaceful living prepare youth to live in ways that are intentional and responsive to the needs of others. Learning and teaching for peace is a life-long journey. Literature can inspire positive change and be a guide in preparation for that pursuit. Ideally, every child would have early experiences that lay a foundation for peaceful living. However, it is important to note that many young children do not have opportunities to develop orientations toward peace, nor skills for peaceful interactions. They have exposure to biased perspectives and ongoing violence, without experience with peaceful alternatives. For those children to learn peaceful ways of living, regardless of age, going back to the beginning is essential. The developmental framework presented in this chapter addresses children's needs for orientations and skills of peaceful living. Fortunately, diverse literature is available for every age group to affirm personal and social identities while promoting understanding and respect for others. Through those stories they learn the language, perspectives, and skills that promote harmonious relationships and conflict transformation. With support from caring adults youth can grapple with difficult conflicts and realize their potential for contributing to positive change.

Featured Literature

The chart below presents the Lexile reading levels for the youth literature featured in this book. The Lexile Framework for Reading (MetaMetrics, 2014) indicated the Lexile level for each text. While the chart includes all of the texts featured in this book, the indication of Lexile levels represents the available information in the Lexile database at the time of this writing. Titles missing information about their Lexile level have the classification in the chart as Unknown.

The Lexile levels signify difficulty of reading based on analysis of syntactic and semantic elements and they serve as a selection guide for literature that children will independently read. Lexile analysis does not take into account a reader's background knowledge or interests, nor does it consider the complexity of the presented issues. Many of the books with higher readabilities hold instructional images and ideas for use with younger children through read aloud and discussion. Likewise, the lower-level books stimulate thinking and communication about difficult peace issues among older and higher-level readers. The authors of this book have much experience with both uses of youth literature for peace education. They recommend preview and careful selection of quality literature that meets the individual and group needs of youth.

Author	Title	Lexile
Adler, D. A.	*Heroes for Civil Rights*	970L
Agassi, M.	*Hands Are Not For Hitting*	Unknown
Ajmera, M., Omolodun, O., & Strunk, S.	*Extraordinary Girls*	Unknown
Alexie, S.	*The Absolutely True Diary of a Part-time Indian*	600L
Archibold, F.	*The Sandbox*	Unknown
Asim, J.	*Whose Knees Are These?*	Unknown
Atgwa, J., Bakyayita, J., & Boltauzer, J.	*Stand Up for Your Rights*	Unknown
Atkins, J.	*Aani and the Tree Huggers*	650L
Barakat, I.	*Tasting the Sky: A Palestinian Childhood*	870L
Baskwill, J.	*If Peace Is*	540L
Bausum, A.	*With Courage and Cloth: Winning the Fight for a Woman's Right to Vote*	1080L
Beaumont, K.	*I Like Myself*	Unknown
Bedford, D.	*It's My Turn*	Unknown
Berry, J. W.	*Mine & Yours: Human Rights for Kids*	600L
Birth, B.	*Lucky Beans*	Unknown
Blacksheep, B.	*Baby Learns about Colors*	680L
Boelts, M.	*Those Shoes*	750L
Borden, L.	*The Greatest Skating Race: A World War II Story from Netherlands*	780L
Boughman, A.	*Chicora and the Little People: The Legend of Indian Corn, A Lumbee Tale*	Unknown
Bowen, C.	*I Can Believe in Me: A Book of Affirmations*	1080L
Boyne, J.	*The Boy in the Striped Pajamas*	Unknown
Braun, S.	*Women Inventors Who Changed the World*	Unknown

Author	Title	Level
Brennen, S. S.	Uncle Bobby's Wedding	530L
Broker, J.	Night Flying Woman: An Ojibway Narrative	Unknown
Brown, L. K.	How to Be a Good Friend	Unknown
Brown, M.	Side by Side/Lado a lado: The Story of Dolores Huerta and Cesar Chavez/ La historia de Dolores Huerta y Cesar Chaves	870L
Bruchac, J.	Code Talker: A Novel about the Navajo Marines of World War Two	910L
Bruchac, J.	Hidden Roots	830L
Buckley, H. E.	Grandfather and I	490L
Bunting, E.	Going Home	480L
Bunting, E.	One Green Apple	450L
Bunting, E.	Terrible Things: An Allegory of the Holocaust	Unknown
Burgess, M.	Billy Elliot	520L
Buss, F. L.	Journey of the Sparrow	760L
Byers, A.	Saving the Children from the Holocaust: The Kindertransport	850L
Cain, J.	The Way I Feel	Unknown
Cali, D. & Bloch, S.	The Enemy: A Book About Peace	Unknown
Camp, C. A.	American Women Inventors: Collective Biographies	1030L
Campbell, N. I.	Shi-shi-etko	Unknown
Campbell Bartoletti, S.	Growing Up in Coal Country	1110L
Capaldi, G.	A Boy Named Beckoning: The True Story of Dr. Carlos Montezuma, Native American Hero	880L
Carle, E.	The Grouchy Lady Bug	560
Carlson, N. S.	The Family Under the Bridge	680L
Carnes, J.	Us and Them: A Story of Intolerance in America	Unknown
Carter, J.	Talking Peace, a Vision for the Next Generation	Unknown

continued

Author	Title	Lexile
Carvell, M.	Who Will Tell My Brother?	Unknown
Carvell, M.	Sweetgrass Basket	1000L
Castle, C.	For Every Child: The Rights of the Child in Words and Pictures	Unknown
Child, L.	I've Won, No I've Won, No I've Won	Unknown
Chin-Lee, C.	Akira to Zoltan: Twenty-six Men Who Changed the World	Unknown
Christie, C.	All My Friends Are Different but We Are All the Same	Unknown
Clifton, L.	Everett Anderson's Goodbye	1050L
Clifton, L.	Everett Anderson's Friend	Unknown
Cohen, D. B.	Papa Jethro	Unknown
Cole, K.	No Bad News	730L
Coles, R.	The Story of Ruby Bridges	Unknown
Cottin, M.	The Black Book of Colors	570L
Couric, K.	The Brand New Kid	810L
Craighead, G. J.	My Side of the Mountain	750L
Curtis, C. P.	The Mighty Miss Malone	Unknown
Dauvillier, L.	Hidden: A Child's Story of the Holocaust	810L
DeFelice, C.	One Potato, Two Potato	990L
Deloria, E. C.	Waterlily	980L
Demi	Gandhi	400L
DePaolo, T.	Trouble in the Barker's Class	570L
DiSalvo, D.	A Castle on Viola Street	Unknown
Dungy, T.	You Can Do It!	930L
Ehrlich, A.	Rachel: The Story of Rachel Carson	

Ellis, D.	The Breadwinner	630L
Elvgren, J.	The Whispering Town	Unknown
Finkelstein, N. H.	Remember Not to Forget	830L
Fradin, D.	September 11, 2001	Unknown
Freedman, R.	Freedom Walkers: The Story of the Montgomery Bus Boycott	1110L
Freedman, R.	Kids at Work: Lewis Hine and the Crusade against Child Labor	1140L
Fox, M.	Ten Little Fingers and Ten Little Toes	Unknown
Gransworth, E.	If I Ever Get Out of Here	870L
Gilchrist, C.	Stories from the Silk Road	860L
Gilley, J.	Peace One Day	Unknown
Glaser, L.	Emma's Poem: The Voice of the Statue of Liberty	790L
Global Fund for Children	Global Babies	Unknown
Greenfield, E.	When the Horses Ride By	Unknown
Gugler. L. D.	A Piece of Forever	Unknown
Hamilton, V.	If the People Could Fly: American Black Folktales	660L
Haskins, J.	Delivering Justice: W. W. Law and the Fight for Civil Rights	Unknown
Herron, C.	Always an Olivia: A Remarkable Family History	Unknown
Herumin, W.	Child Labor Today: A Human Rights Issue	Unknown
Hesse, K	Spuds	810L
Hill, L.	Dave the Potter: Artist, Poet, slave	1100L
Hinton, S. E.	The Outsiders	750L
Hoffman, E.	Play Lady	Unknown
Hoffman, M.	The Colour of Home	540L
Hoffman, S.	Jacob's New Dress	Unknown

continued

Author	Title	Lexile
Hoose, P.	Claudette Colvin: Twice Toward Justice	Unknown
House, S. & Vaswani, N.	Same Sun Here	890L
Howe, J.	The Misfits	960L
Hubbard, J.	Lives Turned Upside Down: Homeless Children in Their Own Words	Unknown
Hudson, W.	Black Heroes: Scientists, Healers, and Inventors	Unknown
Hutchins, P.	The Doorbell Rang	340L
Isadora, R.	What a Family	Unknown
Jackson, C.	Playground: The Mostly True Story of a Former Bully	Unknown
Jimenez, F.	The Circuit: Stories from the Life of a Migrant Child	880L
Jimenez, K. P.	Are You Are a Boy or a Girl?	Unknown
Johnson, A.	When I Am Old with You	730L
Johnson, J. C.	Seeds of Change: Planting to a Path of Peace	820L
Johnston, T.	Angel City	650L
Johnston, Y.	The Harmonica	620L
Joosse, B.	Stars in the Darkness	Unknown
Katz, K.	Can You Say Peace	260L
Kelly, J.	The Evolution of Calpurnia Tate	830L
Kerley, B.	A Little Peace	830L
Kerley, B.	One World One Day	400L
Kielburger, C.	Free the Children	Unknown
Kimmel, E. C.	Ladies First: 40 Daring American Women Who Were Second to None	Unknown
King, M. L.	My Daddy, Dr. Martin Luther King, Jr.	680L

Author	Title	Level
Krass, P.	Sojourner Truth: Antislavery Activist	Unknown
Krull, K.	Harvesting Hope: The Story of Cesar Chavez	800L
Kurtz, J.	Faraway Home	610L
Landowne, Y.	S'elavi, That is Life: A Haitian Story of Hope	660L
Lasky, K.	John Muir: America's First Environmentalist	Unknown
Lee-Tai, A	A Place Where Sunflowers Grow	790L
Leitich Smith, C.	Indian Shoes	820L
Leitich Smith, C.	Rain Is Not My Indian Name	860L
Lietich Smith, C.	Jingle Dancer	710L
Levinson, C.	We've Got a Job: The 1962 Children's March	1020L
Lexington, C.	Bear Learns to Share	Unknown
Littlefield, H.	Fire at the Triangle Factory	400L
Loewen, N.	No Fair: Kids Talk about Fairness	640L
Lord, M.	A Song for Cambodia	840L
Loyie, L.	As Long as the Rivers Flow: A Last Summer Before Residential School	Unknown
Ludwig, T.	Confessions of a Former Bully	810L
Lyon, G. E.	You and Me and Home Sweet Home	530L
MacLachan, P.	Through Grandpa's Eyes	560L
Markel, M.	Brave Girl: Clara and the Shirtwaist Makers Strike of 1909	760L
Martin, C.	Mohandas Gandhi	950L
Mayer, M.	I Was So Mad	430L
Mayer, P.	Don't Sneeze at the Wedding	Unknown
McBratney, S.	I'm Sorry	Unknown
McBratney, S.	Guess How Much I Love You	690L
McDermott, G.	Arrow to the Sun	480L

continued

Author	Title	Lexile
McGovern, A.	*The Lady in the Box*	370L
McKissack, P.	*Goin' Someplace Special*	550L
McQuinn, A.	*Lola Loves Stories*	580L
Medina Wordsong, A.	*The Dream on Blanca's Wall/El Sueno Pegado en la Pared de Blanca: Stories in English and Spanish*	Unknown
Meiners, C. J.	*Talk and Work It Out*	Unknown
Meiners, C. J.	*Cool Down and Work Through Anger*	Unknown
Messaoudi, M.	*My Mum is a Wonder*	Unknown
Messinger, C.	*When the Shadbush Blooms*	860L
Miller, W.	*Rent Party Jazz*	820L
Milway, K. S.	*One Hen: How One Small Loan Made a Big Difference*	810L
Mitchell, M. K.	*Uncle Jed's Barbershop*	710L
Mobin-Uddin, A.	*The Best Eid Ever*	670L
Mochizuki, K.	*Baseball Saved Us*	550L
Mora, P.	*Tomas and the Library Lady*	440L
Mora, P.	*Pablo's Tree*	410L
Monceaux, M. & Katcher, R.	*My Heroes, My People: African Americans and Native Americans in the West*	1120L
Morris, A.	*Families*	40L
Mortenson, G. & Roth. S.	*Listen to the Wind: The Story of Dr. Gregg and Three Cups of Tea*	740L
Moss, P.	*Say Something*	430L
Mundy, M.	*Mad Isn't Bad: A Child's Book about Anger*	Unknown
Munoz Ryan, P.	*Esperanza Rising*	750L
Munoz Ryan, P.	*When Marian Sang: The True Recital of Marian Anderson*	780L

Author	Title	Level
Myers, W.	Ida B. Wells: Let the Truth Be Told	900L
Myers, W. D.	The Young Landlords	820L
Myacle, L.	Luv Ya Bunches	710L
Newman, L.	Daddy, Pappa, and Me	Unknown
Newman, L.	Mommy, Mama, and Me	Unknown
Nivola, C. A.	Planting the Trees of Kenya: The Story of Wangari Maathai	1030L
Nolan, A.	What I Like About Me!	Unknown
Nolan, J.	In My Momma's Kitchen	530L
Nothman, S.	Give It Back!	Unknown
O'neil, A.	The Recess Queen	450L
Onyefulu, I.	Ogbo: Sharing Life in an African Village	950L
Orgel, D.	The Devil in Vienna	700L
Orgill, R.	If I Only Had a Horn	860L
Ortiz, S.	The People Shall Continue	540L
Oxenbury, H.	I Can	Unknown
Oxenbury, H.	I See	Unknown
Oxenbury, H.	I Touch	Unknown
Parker, M. J.	Wild and Wooly	Unknown
Parr, T.	The Best Friends Book	Unknown
Parr, T.	We Belong Together	Unknown
Parr, T.	I Love You Just Because	Unknown
Parr, T.	The Feel Good Book	Unknown
Parr, T.	The I Love You Book	230L
Parr, T.	The Peace Book	Unknown
Parr, T.	The Okay Book	Unknown

continued

Author	Title	Lexile
Patterson, K.	Bridge to Terabithia	810L
Payne, L. M.	We Can Get Along: A Child's Book of Choices	Unknown
Peck, J. & Davis, D.	The Green Mother Goose: Saving the World One Rhyme at a Time	Unknown
Perez, A.	My Diary from Here to There	720L
Peterson, J. W.	I Have a Sister—My Sister is Deaf	520L
Pinkney, A.	Sit-in: How Four Friends Stood Up by Sitting Down	500L
Pinkney, A.	Let It Shine: Stories of Black Women Freedom Fighters	940L
Pinkney, A.	Sojourner Truth's Step-Stomp Stride	650L
Polacco, P.	January's Sparrow	760L
Polacco, P.	Mr. Lincoln's Way	450L
Queen Rania of Jordan	The Sandwich Shop	630L
Radunsky, V.	What Does Peace Feel Like?	Unknown
Raven, M. T.	Mercedes and the Chocolate Pilot	850L
Rawlings, M. K.	The Secret River	720L
Rogers, F.	Making Friends	Unknown
Rylant, C.	When I Was Young in the Mountains	980L
Santiago, C. & Lowry, J.	Home to Medicine Mountain	520L
Saenz, B. A.	A Gift from Papa	Unknown
Sanderson, E.	Two Pairs of Shoes	Unknown
Sapp, A.	Music for Alice	Unknown
Schaefer, L. A.	Some Kids Are Blind	470L
Schafer, L. A.	Some Kids Are Deaf	500L

Schafer, L. A.	Some Kids Wear Leg Braces	510L
Schafer, L. A.	Some Kids Use Wheel Chairs	440L
Schindler, H.	The Junction of Sunshine and Lucky	Unknown
Schroeder, A.	Ragtime Tumpie	610L
Scholes, K.	Peace Begins with You	840L
Schuett, S.	Somewhere in the World Right Now	550L
Serres, A.	I Have the Right to Be a Child	Unknown
Seuss, D.	Yertle the Turtle and Other Stories	520L
Sornson, B.	Stand in My Shoes: Kids Learning about Empathy	Unknown
Sheth, K.	Keeping Corner	760L
Shin, S. Y.	Cooper's Lesson	Unknown
Siddals, A. W.	Compost Stew: An A to Z Recipe for the Earth	Unknown
Simon, N.	All Families Are Special	Unknown
Simon, N.	All Kinds of Children	Unknown
Soto, G.	Two Many Tamales	670L
Spelman, C. M.	The Way I Feel	Unknown
Spelman, C. M.	When I Care about Others	Unknown
Spelman, C. M.	When I Miss You	Unknown
Spinelli, E.	Peace Week in Miss Fox's Class	480L
Springer, J.	Listen to Us: The World's Working Children	Unknown
Steckel, R. & Steckel, M.	The Milestone Project: Celebrating Children Around the World	Unknown
Steptoe, J.	Baby Says	Unknown
Stevens, J.	The Little Red Pen	300L

continued

Author	Title	Lexile
Sundem, G.	Real Kids, Real Stories, Real Change: Courageous Actions Around the World	980L
Tafolla, C. & Teneyuca, S.	That's Not Fair! Emma Tenayuca's Struggle for Justice/No Es Justo! La lucha de Emma tenayuca por la justicia	590L
Tarple, N. A.	I Love My Hair!	900L
Tate, N.	Down to Earth: How Kids Feed the World	1170L
Taylor, M.	The Well	760L
Taylor, S.	All-of-a-Kind Family	600L
Terkel, S. N.	People Power: A Look at Nonviolent Action and Defense	Unknown
Tichi, C.	Civic Passions: Seven Who Launched Progressive America and What They Teach Us	Unknown
Tingle, T.	Crossing Bok Chitto: A Choctaw Tale of Friendship and Freedom	800L
Tingle, T.	How I Became a Ghost	480L
Tonatiuh, D.	Pancho Rabbit and the Coyote: A Migrant's Tale	Unknown
Tutu, D. & Abrams, D. C.	Desmond and the Very Mean Word	Unknown
Verdick, E.	How to Take the GRRRR Out of Anger	730L

Author	Title	Level
Verdick, E.	Words Are Not for Hurting	200L
Verdick, E.	Sharing Time	Unknown
Voight, C.	Homecoming	630L
Wadsworth, G.	Benjamin Banneker: Pioneering Scientist	550L
Warren, S. E.	Dolores Huerta: A Hero to Migrant Workers	520L
Weatherford, C. B.	Freedom on the Menu	660L
Welch, C.	Children of the Civil Rights Era	Unknown
Wheeler, B.	Where Did You Get Your Moccasins?	Unknown
Wilhelm, H.	I Won't Share	Unknown
Williams, S. A.	Working Cotton	600L
Wilson, J.	One Peace: True Stories of Young Activists	Unknown
Winthrop, E.	Counting on Grace	760L
Winter, J.	Follow the Drinking Gourd	630L
Winter, J.	The Librarian of Basra: A True Story from Iraq	640L

References

Ackerman, A. (2003). The idea and practice of conflict prevention. *Journal of Peace Research, 40*(3), 339–347.
Adams, M., Bell, L. A., & Griffin, P. (2007). *Teaching for diversity and social justice* (2nd ed.). New York: Routledge.
Adams, S. K., & Wittmer, D. S. (2001). "I had it first": Teaching young children to solve problems peacefully. *Young Children, 77,* 10–16.
Agarwal-Rangnath, R. (2013). *Social studies, literacy and social justice in the common core classroom: A teacher's guide.* New York: Teachers College.
Alonso, H. H. (1995). One woman's journey into the world of women's peace history. *Women's Studies Quarterly, 23*(3/4), 170–192.
Alpargu, M., Sahin, E., & Yazici, S. (2009). Teaching history and its contributions to peace. *International Journal of Social Inquiry, 2*(2), 199–214.
Andrzejewski, J., Pedersen, H., & Wicklund, F. (2009). In J., Andrzejewski, M, Baltodano, & L. Symcox, (Eds), *Social justice, peace, and environmental education: Transformative standards* (pp. 136–158). New York: Routledge.
Anti-Defamation League. (2014). A world of difference. Retrieved from http://www.adl.org/education-outreach/anti-bias-education/c/a-world-of-difference.html
Apple, M. W. (1995). *Education and power* (2nd ed.). New York: Routledge.
Arizpe, E., & Stules, M. (2003). *Children reading pictures: Interpreting visual texts.* New York: Routledge.
Armstrong, J. (2003). Narrative and violence. *The Horn Book Magazine.* Retrieved from http://archive.hbook.com/magazine/articles/2003/mar03_armstrong.asp.
Arthur, J., & Davison, J. (2000). Social literacy and citizenship education in the school curriculum. *Curriculum Journal, 11*(1), 9–23. doi:10.1080/095851700361366.
Ashley, L. (2008). The language of violence. *Peace Studies Journal, 2*(1), 76–84.

Asia-Pacific Centre of Education for International Understanding. (Ed.). (2008). *Teachers training manual for learning to live together: Education for international understanding and education for sustainable development*. Seoul, Korea: Seunghwan Lee. Retrieved from: http://www.ias.unu.edu/resource_centre/UNU%20IAS%20and%20APCEIU%20teachers%20training%20manual%20on%20EIU%20and%20ESD.pdf.

Avgerinou, M., & Pettersson, R. (2011). Toward a cohesive theory of visual literacy. *Journal of Visual Literacy, 30*(2), 1–16.

Aware Girls. (2012). Promoting peace activism, tolerance and nonviolence. Retrieved from http://www.awaregirls.org/portfolio/gender-mainstreaming-of-peace-buildingpeace/.

Bahador, B. (2012). Rehumanizing enemy images: Media framing from war to peace. In K. V. Korostelina (Ed.), *Forming a culture of peace: Reframing narratives of intergroup relations, equity and justice* (pp. 195–212). New York: Palgrave Macmillan.

Bair, S., Williams, L., & Meghan, F. (2008). Integrating women's history into an early American history course: Three lesson ideas. *Social Studies, 99*(4), 174–180.

Bajaj, M. (2008). Critical peace education. In M. Bajaj (Ed.), *Encyclopedia of peace education* (pp. 135–146). Charlotte, NC: Information Age.

Bajaj, M., & Chiu, B. (2009). Education for sustainable development as peace education. *Peace & Change, 34*(4), 441–455. doi:10.1111/j.1468-0130.2009.00593.

Banks, J. A. (1997). *Teaching strategies for ethnic studies* (6th ed.). Boston, MA: Allyn and Bacon.

———. (1999). *An introduction to multicultural education* (2nd ed.). Boston, MA: Allyn and Bacon.

———. (2003). Teaching literacy for social justice and global citizenship. *Language Arts, 81*(1), 18–19.

Banks, J. A., & McGee, C. A. (2008). *Multicultural education: Issues and perspectives* (2nd ed.). Needham Heights, MA: Simon and Schuster.

Bar-Tal, D. (2002). The elusive nature of peace education. In G. Saloman & B. Nevo (Eds.), *Peace education: The concept, principles, and practices around the world* (pp. 27–36). Mahwah, NJ: Lawrence Erlbaum Associates.

Barton, D., Hamilton, M., & Ivanic, R. (Eds.). (2000). *Situated literacies: Reading and writing in context*. New York: Routledge.

Bass, C. (2005). Learning to love the motherland: Educating Tibetans in China. *Journal of Moral Education, 34*(4), 433–449.

Beaty, J. J. (1996). *Building bridges with multicultural picture books: For children 3–5*. Upper Saddle River, NJ: Prentice Hall.

Bedi, J. E. (2005). Innovative lives. Exploring the history of women inventors. *Smithsonian Institution*. Retrieved from http://invention.smithsonian.org/centerpieces/ilives/womeninventors.html.

Bertling, J. (2013). Exercising the ecological imagination: Representing the future of place. *Art Education, 66*(1), 33–39.
Bigelow, B., Harvey, B. Karp, S., & Miller, L. (Eds.). (2001). *Rethinking our classrooms, Volume 2: Teaching for equity and justice*. Williston, VT: Rethinking Schools.
Biles, B. (1994). Activities that promote racial and cultural awareness. *Family Child Care Connections, 4*(3), 1–7. Retrieved from http://web.aces.uiuc.edu/vista/pdf_pubs/CHLDCARE.PDF.
Bix, A. S. (2010). Beyond Amelia Earhart: Teaching about the history of women aviators. *Organization of American Historians Magazine of History, 24*(3), 39–44.
Björkdahl, A. (2012). A gender-just peace? Exploring the Post-Dayton peace process in Bosnia. *Peace & Change, 37*(2), 286–317.
Bledow, R., Rosing, K., & Frese, M. (2013). A dynamic perspective on affect and creativity. *Academy of Management Journal, 56*(2), 432–450.
Boersema, D., & Brown, K. G. (2006). *Spiritual and political dimensions of nonviolence and peace*. Amsterdam: Rodopi.
Boulding, E. (2000). *Cultures of peace: The hidden side of history*. Syracuse, NY: Syracuse University.
———. (2000). A new chance for human peaceableness? *Peace and Conflict: Journal of Peace Psychology, 6*(3), 193–215. doi:10.1207/S15327949PAC0603_2.
Bourdieu, P., & Passeron, J. C. (1977). *Reproduction in education, society and culture*. Thousand Oaks, CA: Sage.
Bynoe, L. (2004). Strategies for teaching caring and empowerment: Drawing from African American, Mexican American, and Native American traditions. In R. Eisler & R. Miller (Eds.) *Education for a culture of peace* (pp. 189–204). Portsmouth, NH: Heinemann.
Brandt, R. (1994). On educating for diversity: A conversation with James A. Banks. *Educational Leadership, 51*(8), 28–31.
Brashears, K. (2012). Appalachian picturebooks, read-alouds, and teacher-led discussion: Combating stereotypes associated with the Appalachian Region. *Childhood Education, 88*(1), 30–35. doi:10.10 80/00094056.2012.643714.
Braus, N., & Geidel, M. (2000). *Everyone's kids' books: A guide to multi-cultural, socially conscious books for children*. Brattleboro, VT: Everyone's Books.
Brindley, R., & Laframboise, K. L. (2001). The need to do more: Promoting multiple perspectives in preservice teacher education through children's literature. *Teaching and Teacher Education, 18*, 405–320.
Bronfenbrenner, U. (1979). *The ecology of human development*. Cambridge, MA: Harvard University Press.
Brunn, S. D., & Yanarella, E. (1987). Towards a humanistic political geography. *Studies in Comparative International Development, 22*(2), 3–49. doi:10.1007/BF02717350.

Brunson, R., Conte, Z., & Masar, S. (2002). *The art in peacemaking: A guide to integrating conflict resolution education into youth arts programs*. Springfield, IL: National Center for Conflict Resolution Education.
California Department of Education. (2005). *History-social science framework for California public school kindergarten through grade twelve* (Rev. ed.). Author. Retrieved from http://www.cde.ca.gov/re/pn/fd/documents/hist-social-sci-frame.pdf.
Carozza, P. M., & Heirsteiner, C. L. (1982). Young female incest victims in treatment: Stages of growth seen with a group art therapy model. *Clinical Social Work Journal, 10*(3), 165–175.
Carter, C. C. (2002). Conflict resolution at school: Building compassionate communities. *Social Alternatives, 21*(1), 49–55.

———. (2003). Prosocial music: Empowerment through aesthetic instruction. *Multicultural Perspectives, 5*(4), 38–40.

———. (2004). Whither social studies? In pockets of peace at school. *Journal of Peace Education, 1*(1), 77–87. doi:10.1080/1740020032000178311.

———. (2008). Voluntary standards for peace education. *Journal of Peace Education, 5*(2), 141–155. doi:10.1080/17400200802264347.

———. (Ed.). (2010). *Conflict resolution and peace education: Transformations across disciplines*. New York: Palgrave Macmillan.

———. (2012). Restorative practices as formal and informal education. *Journal of Peace Education, 9*(2), 1–15. doi.org/10.1080/17400201.2012.721092.

———. (2013, June). *Government standards for peace education: Puzzling the pieces of prescribed pedagogy*. Paper presentation at the XV Comparative Education World Congress. Buenos Aires, Argentina.

———. (2014, April). *Paths to peace education: Biographical comparisons across generations*. Paper presented for the Peace Education Special Interest Group at the annual meeting of the American Educational Research Association, Philadelphia, PA.
Cavanagh, T. (2009). Creating a new discourse of peace in schools: Restorative justice in education. *Journal for Peace and Justice Studies, 18*(1/2), 62–85. doi:10.5840/peacejustice2009181/25.
Center for Nonviolent Communication. (2014). *Feelings inventory*. Retrieved from http://www.cnvc.org/Training/feelings-inventory.

———. (2013). *Needs inventory*. Retrieved from http://www.cnvc.org/Training/needs-inventory.
Chavez-Garcia, M. (2013). The interdisciplinary project of Chicana history: Looking back, moving forward. *Pacific Historical Review, 82*(4), 542–565.
Chen, F., & Yu, S. (2006). Asian North-American children's literature about the Internment: Visualizing and verbalizing the traumatic thing. *Children's Literature in Education, 37*(2), 111–124. DOI 10.1007/s10583-006-9001-9.

Ching, S. H. D. (2005). Multicultural children's literature as an instrument of power. *Language Arts, 83*(2), 107–117.
Christensen, L. (2009). *Teaching for joy and justice: Re-imagining the language arts classroom.* Miwaukee, WI: Rethinking Schools.
Churchill, W. (2004). *Kill the Indian, save the man: The Genocidal impact of American Indian residential schools.* San Francisco, CA: City Lights.
Cohen-Evron, N. (2005). Students living within violent conflict: Should art educators "play it safe" or face "difficult knowledge"? *Studies in Art Education, 46*(4), 309–322.
Colby, S. & Lyon, A. (2004). Heightening awareness about the importance of using multicultural literature. *Multicultural Education, 11*(3), 24–28.
Collaborative for Academic, Social and Emotional Learning. (2014). Collaborating district initiative. Retrieved from http://casel.org/.
Connolly, P., Smith, A., & Kelly, B. (2002). *Too young to notice? The cultural and political awareness of 3–6 year olds in Northern Ireland.* Belfast, Northern Ireland: Community Relations Council.
Cook, K. E., Earles-Vollrath, T., & Ganz, J. B. (2006). Bibliotherapy. *Intervention in School and Clinic, 42*(2), 91–100.
Copple, C., & Bredekamp, S. (2009). *Developmentally appropriate practice in early childhood programs serving children from birth through age 8.* Washington, DC: National Association for the Education of Young Children.
Costanza, R., Fisher, B., Ali, S., Beer, C., Bond, L., Boumans, R., Snapp, R. (2007). Quality of life: An approach integrating opportunities, human needs, and subjective well-being. *Ecological Economics, 612,* 267–276. doi:10.5194/sapiens-1-11-2008.
Costetti, V. (no date). Nonviolent communication experimental project in primary schools. *Nonviolent Communication Research.* Retrieved from https://www.cnvc.org/sites/cnvc.org/files/NVC_Research_Files/Vilma_Costetti_Nonviolent_Communication_Experimental_Project_in_Primary_Schools.pdf.
Cortright, D. (2008). *Peace: A history of movements and ideas.* Cambridge: Cambridge University.
Creative Associates International. (2013). Life cycle of a conflict. *Conflict Prevention Web.* Retrieved from http://www.creativeassociatesinternational.com/CAIIStaff/Dashboard_GIROAdminCAIIStaff/Dashboard_CAIIAdminDatabase/resources/ghai/understanding.htm.
Critchley, P. (2011). *Pythagoras and the harmony of all things.* Retrieved from http://www.academia.edu/705399/Pythagoras_and_the_Harmony_in_All_Things.
Crocco, M. S. (2011). Teaching about women in world history. *The Social Studies, 102*(1), 18–24.

Crystal, D. (2001). *A dictionary of language* (2nd ed.). Chicago: Chicago Press.
Curti, M. (1985). Reflections on the genesis and growth of peace history. *Peace & Change, 11*(1), 1–18.
Danesh, H. B. (2006). Towards an integrative theory of peace education. *Journal of Peace Education, 3*(1), 55–78.
Danesh, H. B., & Clarke-Habibi, S. (2007). *Education for peace curriculum manual: A conceptual and practical guide* (Vol. 1). Vancouver, Canada: EFP Press.
Darder, A. (2012). *Culture and power in the classroom: Educational foundations for the schooling of bicultural students.* Boulder, CO: Paradigm Publishers.
Dayton, C. H., & Levenstein, L. The big tents of U.S. women's and gender history: A state of the field. *Journal of American History, 99*(3), 793–817.
de Souza, M., Francis, L. J., O'Higgins-Norman, J., & Scott, D. G. (Eds.). (2010). *International handbook of education for spirituality care and wellbeing.* International Handbook of Religion and Education, 3. London: Springer.
Deci, E. L. & Ryan, R. M. (2000). The "what" and "why" of goal pursuits: Human needs and the self-determination of behavior. *Psychological Inquiry: An International Journal for the advancement of Psychological Theory, 11*(4), 227–268.
Dermon-Sparks, L., & Edwards, J. O. (2010). *Anti-bias education for young children and ourselves.* Washington, DC: National Association for the Education of Young Children.
Dewey, J. (1938). *Experience and education.* New York: Collier.
Diamond, L. (1999). *The courage for peace. Daring to create harmony in ourselves and the world.* Berkeley, CA: Conari.
DK Publishing. (2003). *The illustrated Oxford dictionary* (Revised ed.). (2003). New York: Dorling Kindersley.
Duncum, P. (2005). Critical thinking in, about and through visual culture. *Journal of Research in Art and Education, 6*(1), 21–35.
Durkheim, E. (1973). *Moral education: A study in the theory and application of the sociology of education.* Trans. Everette K. Wilson and Herman Schnurer. New York: Free Press.
Eisler, R. (2000). *Tomorrow's children: A blueprint for partnership education in the 21st Century.* Boulder, CO: Westview Press.
Eisler, R., & Miller, R. (Eds.). (2004). *Educating for a culture of peace.* Portsmouth, NH: Heinemann.
Emery, F. L. (2002). *That's me! That's you! That's us! Selected current multicultural books for children and young adults presenting positive, empowering images* (5th ed.). Philadelphia, PA: L. R. E. Graphics & Images.

Evans, R. W., & Saxe, D. W. (Eds.). (1996). *Handbook on teaching social issues* [NCSS bulletin 93]. Washington, DC: National Council for the Social Studies.

Fabrica. [This is the complete name of the author] (2007). To die for. *The Walrus*, 4(10), 75–82.

Fadul, J. A. (2008). The development of the concept of death in children: New insights to children's learning process. *The International Journal of Learning*, 15(10), 123–129.

Feeney, A. (1998). *Have you been to jail for justice?* Retrieved from http://www.annefeeney.com/Pages/jail.html.

Ferrara, N. (2004). *Healing through art: Ritualized space and Cree identity*. Montreal, Quebec, Canada: McGill-Queen's University.

Fields, M. V., Perry, N., & Fields, D. M. (2009). *Constructive guidance and discipline: Preschool and primary education* (5th ed.). Upper Saddle River, NJ: Pearson.

Fish, A. (October 18, 2013). Muhammad Ali's greatest fight: Rumble in the high court. *Huffington Post*. Retrieved from http://www.huffingtonpost.com/andrew-fish/muhammad-alis-greatest-fi_b_4099547.html.

Fletcher, K. L., & Reese, E. (2004). Picture book reading with young children: A conceptual framework. *Developmental Review*, 25(1), 64–103.

Fraser, N. (2003). Social justice in an age of identity politics: Redistribution, recognition and participation. In N. Fraser & A. Honneth (Eds.), *Redistribution or recognition: A political-philosophical debate* (pp. 7–109). London: Verso.

Freeman, J. (1967). *Dr. King marches against the war in Viet Nam, March 1967*. Chicago: University of Illinois. Retrieved from http://www.uic.edu/orgs/cwluherstory/jofreeman/photos/KingAtChicago.html.

Freire, P. (1990). *Pedagogy of the oppressed* (2nd ed). New York: Continuum.

Freire, P. (1998). *Pedagogy of freedom: Ethics, democracy, and civic courage*. (P. Clarke, Trans.). Lanham, MD: Rowman & Littlefield.

Friedman, R. S., & Förster, J. (2010). Implicit affective cues and attentional tuning: An integrative review. *Psychological Bulletin*, 136, 875–893. doi: 10.1037/a0020495.

Galtung, J. (2004). *Transcend and transform: An introduction to conflict work*. Boulder, CO: Paradigm Publishers.

Garcia, C. (2014). Review: Chicora and the little people: The legend of Indian corn, A Lumbee tale. Oyate. Retrieved from http://www.oyate.org/index.php/rss-feed/13-review-chicora-and-the-little-people.

Gartrell, D. (2001). Replacing time-out: Part one—Using guidance to build an encouraging classroom. *Young Children*, 56(6), 36–43.

——— (2006). *A guidance approach for the encouraging classroom* (4th ed.). Albany, NY: Thomson Delmar Learning.

Gavigan, K. W., & Kurtts, S. (2011). Using children's and young adult literature in teaching acceptance and understanding of individual differences. *Morality in Education*, 77(2), 11–16.

Gay, G. (1999). Ethnic identity development and multicultural education. In R. H. Sheets & E. R. Hollins, (Eds.), *Racial and ethnic identity in school practices: Aspects of human development* (pp. 195–212). Mahwah, NJ: Lawrence Erlbaum.

Gay, W. C. (1999). The language of war and peace. In L. Kurtz (Ed.) *Encyclopedia of violence, peace, and conflict*, (Vol. 2), 303–312. San Diego, CA: Academic Press.

Gervay, S. (2004). Butterflies: Youth literature as a powerful tool in understanding disability. *Disability Studies Quarterly*, 24(1). Retrieved from http://dsq-sds.org/article/view/844/1019.

Gibson, K. (2012). Influences on diversity in teacher education: Literature to promote multiple perspectives and cultural relevance. *International Journal for the Scholarship of Teaching and Learning*, 6(1), 1–16. Retrieved from http://digitalcommons.georgiasouthern.edu/cgi/viewcon tent.cgi?article=1322&context=ij-sotl.

Gilligan, C. (1982). *In a different voice: Sex differences in the expression of moral judgment*. Cambridge, MA: Harvard University Press.

Giroux, H.A. (1989). *Schooling for democracy: Critical pedagogy in the modern age*. London: Routledge.

Glazier, J., & Seo, J. (2006). Multicultural literature and discussion as mirror and window? *Journal of Adolescent & Adult Literacy*, 48(8), 698–700.

Global Network. (2014). *Keeping space for peace*. Retrieved from http://www.space4peace.org/.

Goldblatt, R., Elkis-Abuhoff, D., Gaydos, M., Rose, S., & Casey, S. (2011). Unlocking conflict through creative expression. *The Arts in Psychotherapy*, 38(2), 104–108. doi: 10.1016/j.aip.2010.12.006.

Goldstein, L. S. (2004). Emphasizing variety rather than commonality: Educating young children for a culture of peace (pp. 127–135). In R. Eisler & R. Miller (Eds.), *Education for a culture of peace*. Portsmouth, NH: Heinemann.

Gomes de Matos, F. (2003). Applied peace linguistics. *Reading Today, 21(2)*, 18.

Gomes de Matos, F. (2008). Learning to communicate peacefully. In M. Bajaj (Ed.), *Encyclopedia of peace wducation*. New York: Teachers College, Columbia University. Retrieved from http://www.tc.columbia.edu/centers/epe/PDF%20articles/fransisco_communicatepeacefully_13sept09.pdf.

Grant, C. A., & Gibson, M. L. (2013). "The path of social justice": A human rights history of social justice education. *Equity & Excellence in Education*, 46(1), 81–99.

Green Cross International. (2013). *Water for life and peace*. Author. Retrieved from http://www.gcint.org/water-for-life-and-peace.

Greene, N. (1995). Releasing the imagination (1st. ed.). San Francisco, CA: Jossey-Bass.

Hagood, M. C. (2002). Critical literacy for whom? *Reading Research and Instruction, 41*(3), 247–266.

Hakvoort, I., & Hagglund, S. (2001). Concepts of peace and war as described by Dutch and Swedish girls and boys. *Peace and Conflict: Journal of Peace Psychology, 7*(1), 29–44.

Hall, E. T. (1969). *The hidden dimension.* New York: Doubleday.

——— (1976). *Beyond culture.* New York: Anchor Books.

Hall, W. A. (1993, May 16). Teaching peace literacy. *The Baltimore Sun.* Retrieved from http://articles.baltimoresun.com.

Harmony. (n.d.). In *Macmillan's online dictionary.* Retrieved from http://www.macmillandictionary.com/dictionary/british/harmony.

Harris, I., & Morrison, M. L. (2013). *Peace education* (3rd ed.). Jefferson, NC: McFarland.

Hart, S., & Hodson, V. K. (2004). *The compassionate classroom: Relationship based teaching and learning.* Encinitas, CA: Puddle Dancer.

Helen Keller Museum. (2010). Young woman 1904–1924. American Foundation for the Blind. Retrieved from http://braillebug.afb.org/hkgal lery.asp?frameid=33.

Hibing, A. N., & Rankin-Erickson, J. L. (2003). A picture is worth a thousand words: Using visual images to improve comprehension for middle school struggling readers. *The Reading Teacher, 56*(8), 758–770.

Hicks, D. (2002). *Lessons for the future: The missing dimension in education.* New York: Routledge.

——— (2002). *Reading Lives: Working-class children and literacy learning.* New York: Teachers College.

——— (2004). Teaching for tomorrow: How can futures studies contribute to peace education? *Journal of Peace Education, 1*(2), 165–178. doi:10.1080/1740020042000253721.

Hostetter, (2009). Reflections on peace and solidarity in the classroom. *Peace & Change, 34*(4), 504–509.

Howlett, C. F., & Harris, I. (2010). *Books, not bombs. Teaching peace since the dawn of the republic.* Charlotte, NC: Information Age.

Howlett, P., & Howlett, C. F. (2008). A silent witness for peace: The case of schoolteacher Mary Stone McDowell and America at war. *History of Education Quarterly, 48*(3), 371–396. DOI: 10.1111/j.1748-5959.2008.00156.x.

Human Rights Watch (2008), *A violent education: Corporal punishment of children in US schools.* New York: Human Rights Watch. Retrieved from http://www.hrw.org/reports/2008/us0808/us0808web.pdf.

Hutchinson, F. P. (1996). *Educating beyond violent futures.* New York: Routledge.

Hutchinson, F. P., & Herborn, P. J. (2012). Landscapes for peace: A case study of active learning about urban environments and the future. *Futures, 44*(1), 24–35. doi:10.1016/j.futures.2011.08.004.

International Institute for Restorative Practices. (2014). Projects. Retrieved from http://www.iirp.edu/projects.php

Interspecies. (2014). Interspecies communication with whales. Retrieved from http://www.interspecies.com/.

Jane Addams Peace Association. (2014). List all books. *Book Awards*. Retrieved from http://www.janeaddamspeace.org/_books/.

Johnson, D. W., & Johnson, R. T. (1995). Teaching students to be peacemakers: Results of five years of research. *Peace and Conflict: Journal of Peace Psychology, 1*(4), 417–438. doi:10.1207/s15327949pac0104_8.

———. (2009). Effective peace education in the classroom: Creating effective peace education programs. In G. Salomon & B. Nevo (Eds.), *Peace education: The concepts, principles, and practices around the world* (pp. 223–240). Mahwah, NJ: Lawrence Erlbaum.

———. (2010). Peace education in the classroom: Creating effective peace education programs. In G. Salomon & E. Cairns (Eds.), *Handbook on Peace Education* (pp. 223–240). New York: Taylor and Francis.

Kaplan, F. (Ed.). (2007). *Art therapy and social action*. Philadelphia, PA: Jessica Kingsley.

Keen, S. (1986). *Faces of the enemy. Reflections of the hostile imagination*. New York: Harper and Row.

Kendall, F. (2012). *Understanding white privilege: Creating pathways to authentic relationships across race*. New York: Routledge.

Kruse, M. (2001). Escaping ethnic encapsulation: The role of multicultural children's literature. *The Delta Kappa Gamma Bulletin, 67*(2), 26–32.

Laman, T. T. (2006). Changing our minds/changing the world: The power of a question. *Language Arts 83*(3), 203–214.

Landy, S. (2002). *Pathways to competence: Encouraging healthy social and emotional development in young children*. Baltimore, MD: Paul H. Brookes.

Langager, M. (2009). Elements of war and peace in history education in the US and Japan: A case study comparison. *Journal of Peace Education, 6*(1), 119–136.

Lantieri, L., & Patti, J. (1996). *Waging peace in our schools*. Boston, MA: Beacon Press.

Larrick, N. (1965, September 11). The all-white world of children's books [Online PDF version of article]. *The Saturday Review*, 63–65. Retrieved from http://www.unz.org/Pub/SaturdayRev-1965sep11-00063.

Lee, N. (2013). Engaging the pink elephant in the room: Investigating race and racism through art education. *Studies in Art Education, 54*(2), 141–157.

Lederach, J. P. (2005). *The moral imagination: The art and soul of building peace*. Oxford: Oxford University.

Levin, D. (2010). The vital connection between anti-bias education and peace education. In L. Derman-Sparks and J. Olsen Edwards (Eds.), *Anti-

bias education for young children and ourselves (pp.12). Washington, DC: National Association for the Education of Young Children.
Levin, F. (2007). Encouraging ethical respect through multicultural literature. *The Reading Teacher, 61*(1), 101–104. doi:10.1598/RT.61.1.13.
Lewison, M., Flint, A. S., & Van Sluys, K. (2002). Taking on critical literacy: The journey of newcomers and novices. *Language Arts, 79*(5), 382–292.
Library of Congress. (2010). Women of invention: Women inventors and patent holders. *Science reference guides.* Retrieved from http://www.loc.gov/rr/scitech/SciRefGuides/womeninventors.html.
———. (2013). *Women's history month.* Retrieved from http://www.women shistorymonth.gov/.
Lohfink, G. (2012). Promoting self-questioning through picture book illustrations. *Reading Teacher, 66*(4), 295–299.
Lonigan, C. J., Farver, J. M., Phillips, B., & Clancy-Menchetti, J. (2011). Promoting the development of preschool children's emergent literacy skills: A randomized evaluation of a literacy-focused curriculum and two professional development models. *Reading and Writing Quarterly, 24*(3), 305–337. doi:10.1007/slll45-009-9214-6.
MacPhee, D. A., & Whitecotton, E. J. (2011). Bringing the "social" back to social studies: Literacy strategies as tools for understanding history. *The Social Studies, 102*(6), 263–267. doi: 10.1080/00377996.2011.571300.
Madhuri, J., Tao Han, K., & Laughter, J. (2013). Addressing social justice in teacher education through children's literature. *Colorado Reading Journal, 24,* 38–45.
Mahiri, J. (Ed.). (2004). *What they don't learn in school: Literacy in the lives of urban youth.* New York: Peter Lang.
Maguth, B. M., & Hilburn, J. (2011). The community as a learning laboratory: Using place-based education to foster a global perspective in the social studies. *Ohio Social Studies Review, 47*(1), 27–34.
Marshall, G. (1998). A dictionary of sociology. *Encyclopedia.com.* Retrieved from http://www.encyclopedia.com/doc/1088-dominant culture.html.
Maslow, A. H. (1943). A theory of human motivation. *Psychological review, 504*(4), 370–396. doi: 10.1037/h0054346.
Massachusettes Institute of Technology (2004). Dishwashing machine. *Inventor of the Week Archive.* Retrieved from http://web.mit.edu/invent/iow/cochrane.html.
Marter, J. (2013). 10 tips for resolving conflict. *The psychology of success.* PsychCentral. Retrieved from http://blogs.psychcentral.com/success/2013/10/10-tips-for-resolving-conflict/.
Mayton II, D. M. (2009). *Nonviolence and peace psychology: Intrapersonal, interpersonal, social and world peace.* New York: Springer.

McGlynn, C., Zembylas, M., Bekerman, Z., & Gallagher, T. (Eds.). (2009). *Peace education in conflict and post-conflict societies: Comparative perspectives*. New York: Palgrave Macmillan.

McGonegal, J. (2009). *Imagining justice: The politics of postcolonial forgiveness and reconciliation*. Montreal, Quebec, Canada: McGill-Queen's University.

Mendoza. J., & Reese, D. (2001). Examining multicultural picture books for the early childhood classroom: Possibilities and pitfalls. *Early Childhood Research & Practice, 3*(2). Retrieved from http://ecrp.uiuc.edu/v3n2/mendoza.html.

Mercieca, C. (2011). *Peace education: Source of national unity and global harmony*. Transcend Media Service. Retrieved from https://www.transcend.org/tms/?p=12848.

Merriam-Webster's Online Dictionary. (2012). *Harmonious*. Retrieved from http://www.merriam-webster.com/dictionary/harmonious.

MetaMetrics. (2014).The Lexile Framework for Reading. Retrieved at http://www.metametricsinc.com/lexile-framework-reading/

Meyer, N. (2011). Selecting diverse resources of Native American perspective for the curriculum center: Children's literature, leveled readers and social studies curriculum. *Educational Libraries, 34*(1), 123–32.

Miller, C., & Churchryk, P. (Eds.). (1996). *Women of First Nations: Power, wisdom and strength*. Winnipeg, Canada: University of Manitoba.

Miller, R. (Ed.). (1991). *New directions in education: Selections from holistic education review*. Brandon, VT: Holistic Education Press.

Mische, P., & Harris, I. (2008). Environmental peacemaking, peacekeeping, and peacebuilding. In M. Bajaj (Ed.), *Encyclopedia of peace education*. Retrieved from Teachers College, Columbia University website: http://www.tc.edu/centers/epe/entries.html.

Moffett, C. A. (2002). Voices from the field: Using Peace Corps literature. *Educational Leadership, 60*(2), 26–30.

Mok, K. (2009). Women we love: 11 environmental heroines. *Treehugger*. Retrieved from http://www.treehugger.com/culture/women-we-love-11-environmental-heroines-slideshow.html.

Möller, F. (2013). *Visual peace: Images, spectatorship and the politics of violence*. New York: Palgrave Macmillan.

Montessori, M. (1992). *Education and peace* (H. R. Lane, Trans.). Oxford: Clio Press.

Moon, B. L. (2012). *The dynamics of art as therapy with adolescents*. Springfield, IL: Charles C. Thomas Publisher.

Morgan, H. (2009). Picture book biographies for young children: A way to teach multiple perspectives. *Early Childhood Education Journal, 37*(3), 219–227. doi:10.1007/s10643-009-0339-7.

Nadler, A., & Liviatan, I. (2006). Intergroup reconciliation: Effects of adversary's expressions of empathy, responsibility and recipients' trust. *Personality and Social Psychology Bulletin, 32*(4), 459–470.

Nair, G. (n.d.). Peace education and conflict resolution in school. *Health Administrator, The Official Journal of the Indian Society of Health Adminstrators, 17*(1), 38–42.
National Council for the Social Studies. (2014). *A vision of powerful teaching and learning in the social studies: Building social understanding and civic efficacy.* Retrieved from http://www.socialstudies.org/positions/powerful.
Ndura-Quédraogo, E., & Amster, R. (2009). *Building cultures of peace: Transdisciplinary voices of hope and action.* Newcastle upon Tyne, UK: Cambridge Scholars.
Nicholson, J. I., & Person, Q. M. (2003). Helping children cope with fears: Using children's literature in classroom guidance. *Professional School Counseling, 7*(1), 15–19.
Nicoll, F. (2004). Reconciliation in and out of perspective: White knowing, seeing, curating and being at home in and against Indigenous sovereignty. In A. Moreton-Robinson (Ed.), *Whitening race: Essays in social and cultural criticism* (pp. 17–31). Canberra, Australia: Aboriginal Studies.
Nieto, S. (2000). *Affirming diversity: The sociopolitical context of multicultural education* (3rd ed.). New York: Longman.
———. (2006). Affirmation, solidarity and critique: Moving beyond tolerance in education. In E. Lee, D. Menkart, & M. Okazawa-Rey (Eds.), *Beyond heroes and holidays: A practical guide to K-12 multicultural education and staff development* (pp. 18–29). Washington, DC: Teaching for Change.
Noddings, N. (2008). Caring and peace education. In M. Bajaj (Ed.), *Encyclopedia of peace education* (pp. 87–91). Charlotte, NC: Information Age.
———. (2012). *Peace education: How we come to love and hate war.* New York: Cambridge University.
Mische, P., & Harris, I. (2008). Environmental peacemaking, peacekeeping, and peacebuilding. In M. Bajaj (Ed.), *Encyclopedia of peace education.* Retrieved from Teachers College, Columbia University website: http://www.tc.edu/centers/epe/entries.html.
Munoz Ryan, P. (2002). *When Marian sang: The true recital of Marion Anderson.* New York: Scholastic.
Olivius, E. (2011). Humanitarian assistance and the politics of gender equality: A study of refugee camps on the Thai-Burma border. In K. Höglund & H. Fjelde (Eds.), *Building peace, creating conflict? Conflictual dimensions of local and international peacebuilding,* pp. 149–168. Lund: Sweden: Nordic Academic.
Oxford, R. (2013). *The language of peace: Communicating to create harmony.* Charlotte, NC: New Age.
Pahl, K., & Rowsell, J. (2011). Artifactual critical literacy: A new perspective for literacy education. *Berkeley Review of Education, 2*(2), 129–151.

Papagianni, K. (2009). Political transition after peace agreements: The importance of consultative and inclusive political processes. *Journal of Intervention and Statebuilding*, 3(1), 47–63.

Paquette, K. R., & Kaufman, C. C. (2008). Merging civic and literacy skills. *The Social Studies*, 99(4), 187–190.

Pate, G. (1997). Research on reducing prejudice. In M. E. Haas & M. A. Laughlin (Eds.), *Meeting the standards: Social studies readings for K-6 educators* (pp. 91–93). Washington, DC: National Council for the Social Studies.

Peacebuttons. (2014). The year in peace and social justice. *Peacebuttons*. Retrieved from http://www.peacebuttons.info/E-News/peacehistoryindex.htm.

Perini, R. L. (2002). The pearl in the shell: Author's notes in multicultural children's Literature. *The Reading Teacher*, 55(5), 428–431. Retrieved from http://www.jstor.org/stable/20205075.

Piaget, J. (1952). *The origins of intelligence*. New York: International Universities Press.

——— (1966). *The moral judgment of the child*. New York: Free Press.

———. (1971). *The construction of reality in the child*. New York: Ballantine.

Picower, B. (2012). Using their words: Six elements of social justice curriculum design for the elementary classroom. *International Journal of Multicultural Education*, 12(1), 1–17.

Pilgrim, P. (no date). *Steps toward inner peace: Harmonious principles for human living*. Retrieved from http://peacepilgrim.com/pdf-files/Steps.pdf.

Pires, M. (2011). Building identity and understanding diversity: Children's literature and traditional literature potential in the school curriculum. *US-China Education Review*, 251–262. Retrieved from http://files.eric.ed.gov/fulltext/ED528330.pdf.

Plumwood, V. (1993). *Feminism and the mastery of nature*. New York: Routledge. Retrieved from http://uspace.shef.ac.uk/servlet/JiveServlet/previewBody/69058-102-1-133834/Plumwood,%20V.%20(1993)%20Feminism%20and%20the%20Mastery%20of%20Nature.pdf.

Pranis, K. (2005). *The little book of circle processes*. Intercourse, PA: Good Books.

Pratt, R. C. (1890). *Official Report of the Nineteenth Annual Conference of Charities and Correction* (1892), 46–59. Reprinted in Richard H. Pratt, "The Advantages of Mingling Indians with Whites," *Americanizing the American Indians: Writings by the "Friends of the Indian" 1880–1900* (Cambridge, MA: Harvard University Press, 1973), 260–271. Retrieved from http://socrates.bmcc.cuny.edu/bfriedheim/pratt.htm.

Prior, L. A., Willson, A., & Martinez, M. (2012). Picture this: Visual literacy as a pathway to character understanding. *The Reading Teacher*, 66(3), 195–206.
Prothrow-Stith, D., & Spivak, H. R. (2005). *Sugar and spice and no longer nice: How we can stop girls' violence*. San Francisco, CA: Jossey-Bass.
Raggl, A., & Schratz, M. (2004). Using visual to release pupil's voices: Emotional pathways to enhancing thinking and reflecting on learning. In C. Pole (Ed.), *Seeing is believing? Approaches to visual research* (Volume 7). New York: Elsevier.
Raviv, Amiram, Bar-Tal, D., Koren-Silvershatz, L., & Raviv, Alona. (1999). Beliefs about war, conflict and peace in Israel as a function of developmental, cultural and situational factors. In A. Raviv, L. Oppenheimer & D. Bar-Tal (Eds.), *How children understand war and peace* (pp. 161–189). San Francisco: Jossey-Bass.
Rawls, J. (1971). *A theory of injustice*. Cambridge, MA: Belknap Press of Harvard University.
Reardon, B. A. (1988). *Comprehensive peace education: Educating for global responsibility*. New York: Teachers College.
———. (2000). Peace education: A review and projection. In B. Moon, S. Brown, & M. Ben-Peretz (Eds.), *Routledge International Companion to Education* (pp.397–425). New York: Routledge.
Reese, D. (2006). *Gerald McDermott's arrow to the sun*. Retrieved from http://americanindiansinchildrensliterature.blogspot.com/2006/10/ger ald-mcdermotts-arrow-to-sun-gerald.html.
———. (2007). Proceed with caution: Using Native American folktales in the classroom. *Language Arts*, 84(3), 245–246.
Rethinking Schools (2014). Retrieved from www.rethinkingschools.org
Riestenberg, N. (2012). *Circle in the square: Building community and repairing harm in school*. St. Paul, MN: Living Justice.
Robinson, J. O. (2005). No peace without freedom: Race and the Women's International League for Peace and Freedom, 1915–1975. *Journal of American History*, 92(2), 666–668.
Rochman, H. (1993). *Against Borders: Promoting Books for a Multicultural World*. Chicago: American Library Association.
Rogers, M. (1998). Student responses to learning about futures. In D. Hicks & R. Slaughter (Eds.), *Futures education: The world yearbook of education 1998* (pp. 203–216). London: Kogan Page.
Rosenberg, E. (1990). Gender. *The Journal of American History*, 77(1), 116–124.
Rosenberg, M. B. (2003a). *Life-enriching education: Nonviolent communication helps schools improve performance, reduce conflict, and enhance relationships*. Encinitas, CA: PuddleDancer.
———. (2003b). *Nonviolent communication: A language of life*. Encinitas, CA: PuddleDancer.

Rosenberg, M. B. (2005a). *Raising children compassionately: Parenting the nonviolent communication way*. Encinitas, CA: PuddleDancer.
———. (2005b). *Speaking peace in a world of conflict*. Encinitas, CA: PuddleDancer.
Rowsell, J., McLean, C., & Hamilton, M. (2012). Visual literacy as a classroom approach. *Journal of Adolescent & Adult Literacy, 55*(5), 444–447. doi:10.1002/JAAL.00053.
Saeidi, S. (2012). Reconsidering categories of analysis: Possibilities for feminist studies of conflict. *Gender & History, 24*(3), 799–824.
Samantha Smith Foundation. (2014). *Samantha Smith: America's youngest ambassador*. Retrieved from http://www.samanthasmith.info/
Schank, M., & Schirch, L. (2008). Strategic arts-based peacebuilding. *Peace & Change, 33*(2), 217–242.
Schott, L. K. (1997). *Reconstructing women's thoughts: The Women's International League for Peace and Freedom before World War II*. Stanford, CA: Stanford University.
Schwebel, S. (2011). *Child-sized history: Fictions of the past in the U.S. classroom*. Nashville, TN: Vanderbilt University.
Seldin, T. (1999). Holistic peace education. *Montessori Life, 11*(1), 5–47.
Setalvad, T. (2010). Pluralism and transformative social studies "Us and them": Challenges for the Indian classroom. In C. Carter & R. Kumar (Eds.), *Peace philosophy in action* (pp 105–139). New York: Palgrave Macmillan.
Short, K. & Fox, D. (2003). *Stories matter: The complexity of cultural authenticity in children's literature*. Urbana, IL: National Council of Teacher of English.
Simon, L. & Norton, N. E. I. (2011). A mighty river: Intersections of spiritualities and activism in children's and young adult literature. *Curriculum Inquiry, 41*(20, 293–318.
Sinclair, M. (2004). Learning to live together: Building skills and attitudes for the twenty-first century. *Studies in comparative education*. Paris, France: United Nations Educational, Scientific, and Cultural Organization. Retrieved from http://www.ineesite.org/uploads/files/resources/doc_1_48_Learning_to_Live_Together.pdf.
Singer, J. (2006). *Stirring up justice: Writing and reading to change the world*. Portsmouth, NH: Heinemann.
Snauwaert, D. (2011). Social justice and the philosophical foundations of critical peace education: Exploring Nusbaum, Sen, and Freire. *Journal of Peace Education, 8*(3), 315–331. doi:10.1080/17400201.2011.621357.
Spiegel, C. (2010). *Book by book: An annotated guide to young people's literature with peacemaking and conflict resolution themes*. Cambridge, MA: Educators for Social Responsibility.
Spier, E. (2010). Group art therapy with eighth-grade students transitioning to high school. *Art Therapy, 27*(2), 75–83.

Steiner, S. F. (2008). Teaching about peace through children's literature. *In factis pax, 2*(2), 229–244.
Steves, R. (February 1, 2010). Estonia's singing revolution. *Smithsonian.com*. Retrieved from http://www.huffingtonpost.com/andrew-fish/muhammad-alis-greatest-fi_b_4099547.html.
Stomfay-Stitz, A. M. (1993). *Peace education in America, 1828–1990: Sourcebook for education and research.* Metuchen, NJ: Scarecrow.
Stribling, S. (2009). Critical literacy: A building block toward peace. In E. Ndura-Quédraogo and R. Amster (Eds.), *Building cultures of peace: Transdisciplinary voices of hope and action* (pp. 72–84). Newcastle upon Tyne, GB: Cambridge Scholars.
Sunal, C. S., Kelley, K. A., & Sunal, D. W. (2012). What does peace mean? Kindergarteners share ideas. *Social Studies Research and Practice, 7*(2), 1–14.
Swick, K. J., & Freeman, N. K. (2004). Nurturing peaceful children to create a caring world: The role of families and communities. *Childhood Education, 81*(1), 2–8. doi:10.1080/00094056.2004.10521284.
Teaching Tolerance. (2014). Classroom activities. *Teaching Tolerance: A Project of the Southern Poverty Law Center.* Retrieved from http://www.tolerance.org/activities.
Tharp, D. S. (2012). Perspectives: A language for social justice. *Change: The Magazine of Higher Education, 44*(3), 21–23. doi: 10.1080/00091383.2010.672918.
The Alliance for Positive Youth Development, (2013). *Building blocks to outcomes for youth.* Retrieved from http://www.sisgigroup.org/apyd/.
The Earth Charter Initiative. (2014). *The Earth Charter.* Retrieved from http://www.earthcharterinaction.org/content/pages/Read-the-Charter.html.
The Kennedy Center. (n.d.). Reading through the arts: How theater and visual arts can engage students in reading. ArtsEdge, The National Arts and Education Network. Retrieved from http://artsedge.kennedy-center.org/edu cators/how-to/supporting-individual-needs/reading-through-the-arts.aspx.
The New York Department of Education. (2010). *Art as a tool for teachers of English language learners.* Albany, NY: Author.
The Pachamama Alliance. (2014). *About Pachamama.* Retrieved from http://www.pachamama.org/about/accomplishments.
Tiernery, R. (2008). Learning with multiple literacies: Observations of lives exploring meanings, identities, possibilities and worlds. In J. Flood, S. B. Heath, & D. Lapp (Eds.), *Handbook of research on teaching literacy through the communicative and visual arts* (Vol. 2, pp. 101–108). New York, NY: Erlbaum.

Tompkins, G. E. (2007). *Literacy for the 21st century: Teaching reading and writing in pre-kindergarten through grade 4* (2nd ed.). Upper Saddle River, NJ: Pearson.

UNESCO Asia and the Pacific. (1998). *Learning to live together in peace and harmony: Values education for peace, human rights, democracy and sustainable development for the Asia-Pacific region*. Bangkok, Thailand. Author. Retrieved from http://unesdoc.unesco.org/images/0011/001143/114357eo.pdf.

United Nations. (2009). *Convention on the Rights of the Child*. Retrieved from http://www2.ohchr.org/english/bodies/crc/docs/CRC.C.BFA.3-4.pdf

United Nations. (2009). *Convention on the Rights of the Child*. Retrieved from http://www2.ohchr.org/english/bodies/crc/docs/CRC.C.BFA.3-4.pdf.

United Nations General Assembly (1948). *The universal declaration of human rights*. Retrieved from http://www.un.org/en/documents/udhr/.

Van Ausdale, D., & Feagin, J. R. (2001). *The first r: How children learn race and racism*. New York: Rowen & Littlefield.

Vandergrift. K. E. (1996). Female advocacy and harmonious voices: A history of public library services and publishing for children in the United States. In K. P. Smith (Ed.), Imagination and scholarship: The contributions of women to American youth services and literature. *Library Trends, 44*(4), 683–718. doi: 10.1.1.224.465.

Verden, C. E. (2012). Reading culturally relevant literature aloud to urban youths with behavioral challenges. *Journal of Adolescent & Adult Literacy, 56*(7), 619–628.

Vygotsky, L. (1978). *Mind in society: The development of higher psychological processes*. Cambridge, MA: Harvard University Press.

Waldorf Worldwide. (2014). Learning for peace. Fruende der Erziehungskunst Rudof Steiners. Retrieved from http://www.freunde-waldorf.de/en/waldorf-worldwide/organisations-worldwide/israel/shfaram.html.

Walling, D. (2006). Brainstorming themes that connect art and ideas across the curriculum. *Art Education, 59*(1), 18–23.

Wassermann, S. (2000). *Serious players in the primary classroom: Empowering children through active learning experiences* (2nd ed.). New York: Teachers College.

Wedge, J. (2008). *Where peace begins. Education's role in conflict prevention and peacebuilding*. London: International Save the Children Alliance.

Weiner, E. J. (2005). Constructions of innocence in times of war: Breaking into the hegemony of peace. *Taboo: The Journal of Culture & Education, 9*(1), 33–42.

Wenden, A. L. (Ed.). (2004). *Educating for a culture of social and ecological peace*. Albany, NY: State University of New York Press.
Wheeler, E. (2004). *Conflict resolution in early childhood*. Upper Saddle River, NJ: Merrill.
Wichert, S. (1989). *Keeping the peace: Practicing cooperation and conflict resolution*. Philadelphia, PA: New Society Publishers.
Winslow, B., Crocco, M., & Berkin, C. (2009). *Clio in the classroom: A guide for teaching U.S. women's history*. Oxford: Oxford University.
Wolk, S. (2004). Using picture books to teach for democracy. *Language Arts, 82*(2), 26–35.
Wong, S. (2009). Nurturing cultures of peace with dialogic approaches to language and literacy. *TESOL in context: Teaching English to Speakers of Other Languages, 19*(2), 4–17.
Wood, S., & Jocius, R. (2013). Combating "I hate this stupid book!: Black males and critical literacy. *Reading Teacher, 66*(8), 661–669. doi: 10.1002/trtr.1177.
Woods, J. W. (no date). Moses's story: Critical literacy and social justice in an urban kindergarten. *Voices of Practitioners, Teacher Research in Early Childhood Education*, 1–12. Retrieved from https://www.naeyc.org/files/naeyc/file/vop/VoicesWood.pdf.
Woodward, C. Vann. (1989). *The future of the past*. New York: Oxford University Press.
Yogev, E. (2010). History curriculum with multiple narratives. In C. C. Carter & R. Kumar (Eds.), *Peace philosophy in action (pp. 79–104)*. New York: Palgrave Macmillan.
Yokota, J. (1993). Issues in selecting multicultural children's literature. *Language Arts, 70*(3), 156–167.
Yousafzai, M., & Lamb, C. (2013). *I am Malala: The girls who stood up for education and was shot by the Taliban*. London: Orion.
Zajda, J., & Zajda, R. (2002). Reinventing the past to create the future: The rewriting of school history textbooks in post-communist Russia. In M. Schweisfurth, L. Davies and C. Harber (Eds.), *Learning democracy and citizenship: International experiences* (pp. 211–224). Oxford: Symposium Books.
Zierdt, M. (2009). When Native American women first met Europeans. Resource Center, *National Women's History Project*. Retrieved from http://www.nwhp.org/resourcecenter/index.php.

Name Index

Abrams, Douglas C., 95
Ackerman, Alice, 112
Adams, Maurianne, 58, 151
Adams, Suzanne K., 159
Adler, David A., 146
Agarwal-Rangnath, Ruchi, 100, 119
Ajmera, Maya, 45
Alexie, Sherman, 55
Allison, S., 143
Alonso, Harriet H., 123
Alpargu, Mehmet, 136
Amster, Randall, 19
Andrzejewski, Janice, 3
Anti-Defamation League, 9
Apple, Micheal W., 13
Archibold, Tim, 163
Arizpe, Evelyn, 82
Armstrong, Jennifer, 61
Arthur, James, 22
Ashley, Larry, 51, 62, 68, 69, 70, 71, 75, 76
Asia-Pacific Centre of Education for International Understanding, 110
Asim, Jabari, 152
Atgwa, Paul, 76
Atkins, Jeannine, 89
Avgerinou, Maria D., 82
Aware Girls, 108

Bahador, Babak, 96
Bair, Sarah, 131

Bajaj, Monisha, 10, 13
Bakyayita, Jasper, 76
Banks, James A., 31, 44, 48, 58, 151
Barakat, Ibtusam, 78
Bar-Tal, Daniel, 28, 86
Barton, David, 85
Baskwill, Jane, 109
Bass, Catriona, 139
Bausum, Ann, 79, 145
Beaty, Janice J., 150
Beaumont, Karen, 77
Beckerman, Zvi, 22
Bedford, David, 163
Bedi, 131
Bell, L. A., 58, 151
Berry, Joy, W., 76
Bertling, Joy, 98
Biles, Barbara, 32
Birtha, Becky, 160
Bix, Amy Sue, 131
Bjorkdahl, Annika, 125
Blacksheep, B., 152
Bledow, Rondald, 82
Bloch, Serge, 99
Boelts, Maribeth, 160
Boersema, David, 124
Boltauzer, Damien, 76
Borden, Louise, 94
Boughman, Arvis, 64
Boulding, Elise, 14, 98, 134
Bourdieu, Pierre, 13
Boyne, John, 79

Name Index

Brandt, Ron, 58
Brashears, Kathy, 33
Braun, Sandra, 142
Braus, Nancy, 39
Bredekamp, Sue, 45, 152
Brindley, Roger, 74
Broker, Ignatia, 55
Bronfenbrenner, Uri, 152
Brown, Katie. G., 124
Brown, Monica, 161
Bruchac, Joseph, 55, 162
Brunn, Stanley D., 12
Brunson, Russell, 19
Buckley, Helen E., 153
Bunting, Eve, 33, 50, 117
Burgess, Melvin, 154
Buss, Fran L., 49
Byers, Ann, 80
Bynoe, Linda, 45, 58

Cain, Janan, 155
Cali, David, 99
California Department of Education, 12
Camp, Carole A., 142
Campbell, N. I., 55
Campbell Bartoletti, Susan, 164
Capaldi, Gina, 136
Carozza, Phyllis M., 91
Carter, Candice C., 6, 7, 12, 17, 19, 22, 41, 59, 80, 102, 115, 121, 124, 146, 165
Carter, Jimmy, 63
Carvell, Marlene, 50, 55
Casement, Roseanne, 29, 30
Castle, Caroline, 76
Cavanaugh, Tom, 11
Center for Nonviolent Communication, 11, 116
Chavez-Garcia, Miroslava, 131
Chen, Fu-jen, 101
Children of War, 127
Ching, Stuart H. D., 58, 150, 161
Chin-Lee, Cynthia, 133
Chiu, Belinda, 10

Christensen, Linda, 119
Christie, Charlene, 157
Churchill, Ward, 50
Churchryk, Patricia, 19, 131
Clarke-Habibi, Sara, 25, 48
Clifton, Lucille, 155, 163
Cohen, Deborah B., 52
Cohen-Evron, Nurit, 86
Colby, Susan, 44, 54
Cole, Kenneth, 120
Collaborative for Academic, Social and Emotional Learning, 8
Connolly, Paul, 32, 45, 153
Cook, Katherine E., 97
Copple, Carol, 45, 152
Cortright, David, 123
Costanza, Robert, 73
Costetti, Vilma, 116
Cottin, Menena, 77
Craighead George, Jean, 111
Creative Associates International, 132
Critchley, Peter, 128
Crocco, Margaret S., 131
Crystal, David, 21
Curti, Merle, 121
Curtis, Christopher Paul, 37–8

Danesh, H. B., 25, 48
Darder, Antonia, 45, 49, 51, 58, 151
Dauvillier, Loic, 52
Davis, David, 90
Davison, Jon, 22
Dayton, Cornelia H., 131
de Souza, Marian, 9
Deci, Edward L., 73
DeFelice, Cynthia, 160
Deloria, Ella C., 66
Demi, 136
Derman-Sparks, Louise, 32, 46, 51, 150, 151, 161
Dewey, John, 14, 150, 158
Diamond, Louise, 108
DiSalvo, Dyanne, 160

Name Index   203

DK Publishing, 64
Duncum, Paul, 84
Dungy, Tony, 153
Durkheim, Emile, 2

Earth Charter, 87–8
Ehrlich, Amy, 141
Eisler, Riane, 12, 19
Ellis, Deborah, 107
Elvgren, Jennifer, 52
Emery, Francenia L., 29, 121, 152
Evans, Ronald W., 12

Fabrica, 97
Fadul, Jose A., 97
Feagin, Joe R., 45
Feeney, Anne, 99
Ferrara, Nadia, 96
Fields, Marjorie V., 35, 154, 155, 159
Finkelstein, Norman H., 52
Fish, Andrew, 99
Five Step Approach, 159
Fletcher, Kathryn L., 83
Forster, Jens, 82
Fox, Mem, 152
Fradin, Dennis, 137
Fraser, Nancy, 145
Freedman, Russell, 146
Freeman, Nancy K., 7
Freire, Paulo, 13, 45, 58
Friedman, Ronald S., 82
Fugitive Slave Law, 101

Gallagher, Tony, 22
Galtung, Johan, 20, 142, 150
Gandhi, 130, 136, 145
Gansworth, Eric, 78
Garcia, Cora, 64
Gartrell, Dan, 35, 155, 159
Gavigan, Karen W., 97
Gay, Geneva, 67
Gay, William C., 62, 65
Geidel, Molly, 39
Gervay, Susanne, 107

Gibson, Melissa L., 145
Gilchrist, Cherry, 46
Gilley, Jeremy, 126
Gilligan, Carol, 47
Giroux, Henry A., 49
Glaser, Linda, 89
Global Fund for Children, 152
Global Network, 3
Goldblatt, Robert, 91
Goldstein, Lisa A., 49, 58
Gomes de Matos, Francisco, 21, 61, 6, 65, 68, 158, 160
Green Cross International, 127
Greene, Maxine, 98
Greenfield, Eloise, 78
Griffin, P., 58, 151
Gugler, Laurel D., 118

Hagglund, Solveig, 107
Hagood, Margaret C., 84
Hakvoort, Ilse, 107
Hall, Edward T., 51, 68, 70
Hall, Wiley A., 22
Hamilton, Virginia, 78
Han, Tao, 76
Harris, Ian, 10, 134, 149
Hart, Sura, 12
Haskins, Jim, 79
Heirsteiner, Catherine L., 91
Helen Keller Museum, 107
Herborn, Peter J., 14
Herron, Carolivia, 52
Herumin, Wendy, 165
Hesse, Karen, 160
Hibing, Anne N., 82
Hicks, David, 13, 82
Hilburn, Jeremy, 19
Hill, Laban C., 143
Hinton, Susan E., 69
Hodson, Victoria K., 12
Hoffman, Eric, 95
Hoffman, Mary, 81
Hoffman, Sarah, 77
Hoose, Phillip, 79
Hostetter, David, 135

House, Silas, 71
Howe, James, 155
Howlett, Charles F., 124, 134
Howlett, Patricia, 124, 134
Hudson, Wade, 45
Human Rights Watch, 76
Hutchinson Francis, 14, 15

International Institute for Restorative Practices, 11
Interspecies, 10
Isador, Rachel, 87

Jackson, Curtis, 156
Jane Addams Peace Association, 101
Jimenez, Francisco, 47
Jocius, Robin, 121
Johnson, Angela, 153
Johnson, David W., 88, 110
Johnson, Jen C., 126
Johnson Roger T., 88, 110
Johnston, Tony, 153
Joosse, Barbara, 39

Kaplan, Frances, 91
Katcher, Ruth, 162
Katz, Karen, 109
Kaufman, Cathy C., 140
Keen, Sam, 134
Kelly, Jacqueline, 154
Kendall, Francis, 58
Kerley, Barbara, 109, 129
Kielburger, C., 162
King Jr., Martin Luther, 99, 145
Krass, Peter, 145
Kruse, Martha, 48, 49
Kurtts, Stephanie, 97
Kurtz, Jane, 98

Laframboise, Kathryn L., 74
Lamb, Christina, 90
Landowne, Youme, 133
Landy, Sarah, 155
Langager, Mark, 139

Lantieri, Linda, 46, 51, 149
Larrick, Nancy, 29
Lasky, Kathryn, 129
Laughter, J., 76
Lederach, John, 94
Lee, Najuana, 92
Lee-Tai, Amy, 115
Leitich Smith, Cynthia, 156
Levenstein, Lisa, 131
Levin, Diane, 45, 46
Levin, Fran, 29
Levinson, Cynthia, 57
Lewison, Mitzi, 76
Library of Congress, 131, 132
Littlefield, Holly, 165
Liviatan Ido, 94
Lonigan, Christopher J., 83
Lord, Michelle, 126
Loyie, Larry, 50
Ludwig, Trudy, 156
Lyon, S., 44, 54

MacPhee, Deborah A., 140
Madhuri, Marga, 76
Maguth, Brad M., 19
Mahiri, Jabari, 83
Manceaux, Morgan, 162
Markel, Michelle, 165
Marshall, Gordan, 10, 49
Marter, Joyce, 117
Martin, Christopher, 145
Maslow, Abraham H., 73
Massachusetts Institute of Technology, 131
Mayer, Mercer, 74
Mayer, Pamela, 52
Mayton, II, Daniel M., 117
McBratney, Sam, 152, 159
McDermott, Gerald, 56
McGee, Cherry A., 44
McGlynn, Claire, 22
McGonegal, Julie, 94
McKissack, Patricia, C., 120
McQuinn, Anna, 153
Medina Wordsong, J., 154

Name Index 205

Meiners, Cherie J., 158
Mendoza, Jean, 54, 69, 149
Mercieca, Charles, 88
Merriam-Webster's Online Dictionary, 27
Messaoudi, Michele, 153
Messinger, Carla, 55
MetaMetrics, 167
Meyer, Nadean, 140, 141
Miller, Christine, 19, 131
Miller, Ron, 12
Miller, William, 93
Milway, Katie S., 118
Mische, Patricia, 10
Mitchel, Margaret K., 160
Mobin-Uddin, Asma, 111
Mochizuki, Ken, 57
Moffett, Cerylie A., 140
Mok, Kimberley, 128
Moller, Frank, 100
Montessori, Maria, 19, 96
Moon, Bruce L., 91
Mora, Pat, 162
Morgan, Hani, 44, 47, 54, 61
Morris, Ann, 153
Morrison, Mary, L., 149
Mortenson, Greg, 90
Moss, Peggy, 34
Mundy, Michaelene, 155
Munoz Ryan, Pam, 162
Myers, Walter D., 48
Myracle, Lauren, 155

Nadler, Arie, 94
Nair, Gopinath, 110
National Council for the Social Studies, 19
Ndura-Ouedraogo, Elavie, 19
Newman, Leslea, 46, 153
Nicholson, Janice L., 97
Nicoll, Fiona, 94
Nieto, Sonia, 45, 49, 51, 58, 157
Nivoli, Claire A., 79
Noddings, Nel, 11, 132, 150
Nolan, Allia Z., 77

Norton, Nadjwa E. L., 44
Nothman, Shimrit, 159

Olivius, Elisabeth, 125
Omolodun, Olateju, 45
O'neill, Alexis, 158
Onyefulu, Ifeoma, 48
Orgel, Doris, 52
Orgill, Roxane, 132
Ortiz, Sharol, 55
Oxenbury, Helen, 152
Oxford, Rebecca, 62, 65, 67

Papagianni, Katia, 140
Paquette, Kelli R., 140
Parker, Mary J., 113
Parr, Todd, 113, 152, 155, 157
Passeron, J. C., 13
Pate, Glenn, 17
Patterson, Katherine, 35
Patti, Janet, 46, 51, 149
Payne, Lauren, M., 64
Peacebuttons, 146
Peck, Jan, 90
Pedersen, H., 3
Perini, Rebecca L., 47
Person Quinn M., 97
Peterson, Jeanne W., 77
Piaget, Jean, 149, 158, 163
Picower, Bree, 76, 150
Pilgrim, Peace, 88
Pinkney, Andrea, 99, 101, 137
Pires, Maria da Natividade, 44, 58
Plumwood, Val, 128
Polacco, Particia, 79, 108
Pranis, Kay, 85, 115
Pratt, Richard C., 50
Prior, Lori A., 83
Prothrow-Stith, Deborah, 8

Queen Rania of Jordan, 153

Radunsky, Vladimir, 61, 108
Raggl, Andrea, 81
Rankin-Erickson, Joan L., 82

Raven, Margot T., 127
Raviv, Amiram, 86
Rawlings, Marjorie K., 160
Rawls, John, 144
Reardon, Betty A., 9, 16
Reese, Debbie, 53, 54, 55, 56, 69, 149
Reese, Elaine, 83
Rethinking Schools, 12
Riestenberg, Nancy, 115
Robinson, Jo Ann O., 124
Rogers, Fred, 157
Rogers, Martha, 13
Rosenberg, Emily, 140
Rosenberg, Marshall B., 10, 61, 62, 63, 65, 67, 68, 73, 140, 150, 151, 155, 158, 160
Rowsell, Jennifer, 83
Ryan, Richard M., 73
Rylant, Cynthia, 33

Saeidi, Shirin, 140
Saenz, B. A., 63
Sanderson, Esther, 153
Santiago, Chiori, 45
Sapp, J., 67
Saxe, David W., 12
Say, Allen, 102
Schaefer, Lola A., 77
Schank, Michael, 85
Schindler, Holly, 78
Schirch, Lisa, 85
Scholes, Katherine, 62
Schott, Linda K., 123
Schratz, Michael, 81
Schroeder, Alan, 132
Schuett, Stacey, 78
Schwebel, Sarah, 133
Seldin, Tim, 19
Serres, Alain, 76
Setalvad, Teesta, 139
Seuss, Dr., 163
Shin, Sun Y., 117
Siddals, M. M., 89

Simon, Norma, 44, 46
Sinclair, Margaret, 54
Singer, Jessica, 100
Skutch, Robert, 153
Smith, Samantha, 14
Snauwaert, Dale, 13
Sornson, Bob, 155
Soto, Gary, 153
Spelman, Cornelia M., 155
Spiegel, Carol, 134
Spier, Erin, 91
Spinelli, Eileen, 64
Spivak, Howard R., 8
Springer, Jane, 57
Steckel, Michele, 44
Steckel, Richard, 44
Steiner, Stan F., 157
Steptoe, John, 152
Stevens, Janet, 47
Steves, Rick, 99
Stomfay-Stitz, Aline M., 132
Stribling, Stacia, 84
Strunk, Sarah, 45
Stules, Morag, 82
Sunal Cynthia S., 107
Sundem, Garth, 164
Swick Kevin J., 7

Tafolla, Carmen, 59
Tate, Niki, 90
Taylor, Sydney, 52, 153
Teaching Tolerance, 6, 9
Terkel, Susan N., 80
Tharp, D. Scott, 58, 75, 76
The Earth Charter, 87
The Earth Charter Initiative, 88
The New York Department of Education, 84
The Pachamama, Alliance, 144
Tichi, Cecilia, 137
Tiernery, Robert, 85
Tingle, Tim, 48, 101
Tompkins, Gail E., 31
Tonatiuh, Duncan, 78
Tutu, Desmond, 95

Name Index

UNESCO Asia and the Pacific, 110
United Nations, 9, 1, 75, 125, 126
United Nations General Assembly, 75

Van Ausdale, Debra, 45
Vandergrift, Kay E., 128
Vaswani, Neela, 71
Verden, Claire E., 54
Verdick, Elizabeth, 156
Vygotsky, Lev, 32, 45, 149, 153, 158

Wadsworth, Ginger, 162
Waldorf Worldwide, 96
Walling, Donovan R., 100
Warren, Sarah E., 57
Wasserman, Selma, 40
Weatherford, Carole B., 57
Wedge, Joanna, 112, 113
Weiner, Eric J., 139
Welch, Catherine, 146
Wenden, Anita L., 10
Wheeler, Bernelda, 153
Wheeler, Edyth J., 149, 153, 158, 159
Whitecotton, Emily J., 140

Wichert, Susanne, 159
Wicklund, F., 3
Wilhelm, Hans, 163
Williams, Linda, 131
Williams, Sherley, A., 57
Wilson, Janet, 127
Winslow, Barbara, 131
Winter, Jeanette, 136, 142
Winthrop, Elizabeth, 164
Wiviott, Meg, 52
Wong, Shelley, 62
Wood, Summer, 121
Woods, Jeffrey W., 119
Woodson, Jacqueline, 36, 49, 53, 78, 155, 156
Woodward, C. Vann, 124

Yanarella, Ernie, 12
Yogev, Esther, 124
Yokota, Junko, 53
Yousafzai, Malala, 90
Yu, Su-lin, 101

Zalben, Jane B., 126
Zembylas, Michalinos, 22
Zierdt, Margaret, 141
Zolotow, C., 77

Subject Index

activism, 99, 107, 119, 125, 129, 143
ahimsa, 145
anti-Semitism, 52
  See also discrimination
anti-social behaviors, 92
art therapy, 91, 97
artists
  graphic, 92
  performing, 92
arts, 17, 81–103
  conflict prevention, 93
  engagement with, 85
  expression in literature, 81–3
  observation of, 91
  reaction to, 94
  role in peace development, 93, 95, 101
artwork
  effects of, 102
  functions in literature, 81
authentic literature, 45, 54, 60, 78

bias, 33, 45, 50–60
  counteracting, 6, 87
  social, 46
bibliotherapy, 97–8
biography, 101, 107, 132–3, 137, 140–5, 162
books
  picture books, 44, 46, 74
  selection of, 86, 101
bravery, 95, 101, 108, 136, 142

characterization, 28, 41
character(s)
  connection to, 26, 47, 52
  development, 25
  feelings of, 63, 67–9
  flaws, 40
  illustrations of, 35
  messages, 33, 39
  representation of, 35, 38, 46
  traits, 28, 31, 82, 87
citizenship, 136
  global, 13
civil disobedience, 99
civil rights, 79, 99, 137, 146
coexistence, 8–9, 23
cognitive development, 86, 96, 153
coherence, 81–2
collective action, 65, 106–7, 133
communication
  impact on inner peace, 95
  intercultural, 70
  interspecies, 10
  nonviolent, 63, 73
  peaceful, 21, 68
  positive, 159
  verbal, 1
  visual, 1
compassion, 11, 17, 36, 50, 53, 61, 65–8, 71, 73, 87, 151
comprehension, 82–3, 123, 145
conflict
  analysis of, 9, 18, 85, 105, 117, 124, 134

Subject Index

conflict—*Continued*
awareness of, 91
constructive response to, 69, 88
of cultural change, 90
education about, 7–9
internal, 14, 105
interpersonal, 91, 103, 106–7, 110
intrapersonal, 91, 106–8, 122
management, 7–8, 140
occurrence of, 4, 10
prevention, 112
recognition of, 84
resolution, 2, 6, 9
responses to, 4, 7, 10, 20–1, 88, 91, 100, 105, 109, 111–14, 121–3, 130–1, 135, 147
structural, 5, 13–14, 20, 60, 92, 101, 108, 118, 120, 125, 132, 138
systemic, 12–13, 101, 118, 143, 145
transformation, 14, 37, 51, 114, 137, 149–50, 166
violent, 34, 37
connections
personal, 26, 47, 79, 150, 154
text-to-self, 26
text-to-world, 26
culture
contemporary, 29, 33, 44, 51, 55, 102, 109, 133, 165
family, 152
curriculum
hidden, 18
peace-oriented, 56
preparation of, 119
social, 140

Dakota approach, 66
development goals, 92
discrimination, 5, 30, 45, 50, 52, 56–8, 96, 106, 114–15, 120, 124, 135, 161–2

diversity
awareness of, 152
genetic, 90
representation of, 30
dominant culture, 33, 47–9

education
anti-bias education, 45
bully education, 8
holistic education, 96
moral education, 2
multicultural education, 44
secular education, 96
social education, 7–8, 21–2, 134, 138, 140
emotions
negative, 69, 105, 111, 114
empathy, 30, 35, 52–3, 62, 65, 94, 117, 134, 136, 155–6
empowerment, 12–13, 21, 36, 40–1, 125, 163, 165
enmity, 121–2, 133–4
environmentalism, 128
equal opportunities, 99
experiences, 28–30, 123, 139
bully, 156
of children, 44, 54, 129, 136, 141, 151, 154, 159
dominated groups, 52, 55, 58, 151, 162
meaningful learning, 19
personal, 31, 33, 38, 66, 75, 81, 149, 161, 164
vicarious, 47, 64

family, 87, 111, 135, 152–4, 160
support, 107, 132
feelings
about peace, 86, 108
connections between, 64
expressing, 11, 30–1, 83, 159
interpret, 54
Inventory, 11, 116
portrayal of, 113
sensitivity to, 53

Subject Index

unawareness of, 73, 112, 119, 154
understanding, 63, 68, 74, 121, 155–7
females
  problem preventers, 131
feminism, 123, 128
friendship, 3, 8, 48, 101, 156, 165
futurism, 15, 121–2

graphic art, 86, 93
guided discussions, 41, 53, 57, 156

harm
  avoidance of, 4, 17, 53–4, 70, 124, 134, 135
  psychological, 101
  repair of, 10, 35, 71, 92, 114–15, 138
  responses to, 11, 91, 121, 141
harmonious
  actions, 27, 65, 166
  living, 3, 26, 48, 64, 88, 109–10, 128
hegemony, 139
herstory, 8, 89, 123, 137, 141, 147
human interactions, 22, 147
human rights, 9, 13–14, 75–6, 101, 125, 165
humanism, 12, 96
humanity, 3, 10, 28, 34, 88, 113, 150

identity
  authenticity, 55
  clarification, 72, 95–6, 139, 161
  exclusion, 145
  gender, 154
  perceptions of, 59, 65, 153
illustrations, 81
  communication with, 85
  critical analysis of, 86
  identification in, 84, 86
  interactions with, 83
  interpreting, 85
  stimulating senses, 83
sustainability, 89
  for therapy, 91
imagination, 15, 81, 98
inequality, 38, 67, 76, 125
injustice
  awareness of, 28, 30, 164
  normalization of, 118
  response to, 52, 57, 59, 84, 101, 130
  social, 58, 84, 115
instruction
  cross-situational, 17
  explicit, 7
  formal, 6, 18
  informal, 6, 17
  integrative, 18–19
  interdependence, 10
  meaningful, 19
  modeling, 9, 20
  powerful, 19
  rationale, 2, 7
  relevance of, 8
  value-based, 19
intelligence, 32
  social, 22
interdependence, 9–10, 72, 110, 117

justice, 32, 4, 75, 121, 141, 163
  economic, 121, 132
  legal, 4, 27, 99, 144
  social, 4, 27, 36, 56, 76

knowledge, 16, 19, 26, 82
  crucial, 103
  cultural, 51, 54, 93
  historical, 14, 128–9
  linguistic, 82
  nonviolence, 124, 135, 146
  self-awareness, 119
  social, 82, 84

language, 80
  children's communication, 159
  classist, 68, 70

language—*Continued*
compassionate, 65–6
contextual meaning, 70
healing through, 126
invention, 130
listening, 68
of life, 61
nonverbal, 70, 83
nonviolent, 73
of peace, 62
peace linguistics, 21
racist, 68, 70
recognizing, 21
rudimentary form, 91
school mission, 7
sexist, 68, 70
soothing, 151
translations, 21, 95, 111, 116
xenophobic, 68, 70
libraries, 128
literacy
 artistic, 83
 critical, 84, 102, 119
 curriculum integration, 100, 140
 early, 83
 emergent, 82
 herstorical, 123, 131, 137
 historical, 12, 100, 165
 social literacy, 21–2
 visual, 82
literature
 affect from, 82, 138
 appropriate, 165, 167
 artwork in, 81, 102
 authentic, 45, 54–5, 78
 canon, 147
 culturally relevant, 121, 152
 descriptors, 101
 discomforting, 82
 fiction use, 133
 genres, 44
 inauthentic, 56
 inclusive, 86, 149–50
 interaction with, 96, 149

realistic, 47
response to, 130
selection of, 39, 42, 101
sufficient, 141
underrepresented people, 161

memoir, 126
mental images, 98
moral autonomy, 38
motivation, 6, 53, 113, 118, 156

needs
 basic, 28, 78
 expressing, 68, 116
 fulfillment of, 4, 42
 identification of, 63, 127
 intrapersonal, 143
 Inventory, 116
 recognizing, 138
 unfulfilled, 3, 6, 35, 125, 139

oppression, 43, 51, 58, 143
 internalized, 161
 legitimated, 75
 recognition, 13, 58
 structural, 78, 101

pacifism, 2, 107
patriotism
 global, 2
 national, 2, 139
peace
 conception of, 2
 construal of, 2
 creativity, 142
 development, 6, 14, 85, 95, 128
 education, 5, 8, 16
  anti-bias, 45
  coexistence, 8, 43
  comprehensive, 9
  contextual, 19
  empowerment, 12
  legitimating, 124
  pedagogy, 18
  repair of harm, 10

Subject Index 213

skill evaluation, 92
social justice, 144
standards for, 124
sustainable living, 9
visioning, 14
environmental, 3, 10
hidden curriculum, 18, 20
inner, 15, 83, 88–9, 95
interpersonal, 85, 87, 107, 110
interspecies, 3
intrapersonal, 85, 93, 108
language of, 21
mental, 4, 97
movements, 134
negative, 16, 36
outer space, 3, 15, 113
peace-building, 4, 112
pedagogy of peace education, 18
positive, 17, 36
pursuit of, 122, 124, 128, 134
self-actualization, 4
visions, 15
peaceful
actions, 41, 57
living, 72, 149, 151
peacemakers, 6
perceptions, 11, 18, 151
analysis of, 97, 124
care-influenced, 58
contextual, 51, 70
expression of, 82, 94
of others, 6, 50, 65, 67, 77, 86, 124
personal, 130
positive, 29, 64
of power, 32
of self, 86, 152–3
perspective
diversification, 31, 47, 70, 150, 155
philosophy, 128
pluralism, 3, 87, 144
power differential
awareness of, 16, 119
response to, 13

praxis, 143
print awareness, 83
privilege, 51, 58, 118, 120
internalized, 161
problem solving, 63, 116, 131
constructive, 158
counseling as, 11
creativity for, 142

racial integration, 99, 120
racism, 92
recognition of, 124
societal, 38
reflection
collective reflection, 91–2, 114, 133
on emotion, 64
personal reflection, 35, 66, 96, 114
response
analysis of, 18, 144
changing, 91–2
collective, 105
constructive, 69, 72, 88, 143
destructive, 17
empowerment during, 12–13
harm-free, 134, 141
to injustice, 59, 145
need-fulfilling, 42, 138
peace-oriented, 122
potential, 26, 84, 100
proactive, 112, 120, 124
repair, 93
retaliation, 95
role models, 6

satyagraha, 145
schema, 19–20, 32
segregation, 37, 48, 57, 99, 120
self-awareness, 83, 110, 119, 150, 154
self-work, 105, 108
sexism, 84, 87, 101, 124
social activism, 107
social bias, 46, 97

social equality
　desire for, 118
social interactions, 6, 32, 45
social justice. *See* justice
social skills
　culturally conscious, 54
　development, 149
socialization, 65, 87
special needs, 37, 73
spirituality, 18, 95–6
　Navajo, 162
stereotypes, 28–33, 41, 46, 50–1, 60, 102, 160
　gender, 77
storytelling, 20, 94, 101
　healing through, 126
　teaching through, 109
stress relief, 14, 113–15
structural
　problems, 17, 106, 118
　processes, 93, 106
sustainability, 3, 9
　education, 110
　living, 89, 128

understanding, 26, 30–2, 45, 54
　art, 83
　conflict, 39, 68, 122, 138
　cross-cultural, 96
　death, 97
　feelings, 156
　international, 110
　interpersonal, 51, 85
　intrapersonal, 77, 85
　mutual, 27, 43, 54, 65, 150
　social contexts, 149
unity, 2, 48, 68, 96

values, 3
　clarity, 110, 135
　cultural, 66
　different, 51
　gleaning, 109
　modeling, 17
　shared, 28
　terms expressing, 70
violence
　in art, 86
　cross-cultural, 124
　culture of, 135
　elimination of, 10
　exposure, 25, 38, 86, 97, 100, 106, 124, 134
　images of, 97
　perpetuation of, 75, 139
　prevention of, 2, 6, 8, 112–13
　protection from, 94
　renaming, 75
　roots of, 4
visioning, 14, 98
vocabulary
　conflict, 159
　cultural differences, 70
　development, 83
　of feelings, 11
　multilingual, 130
　of needs, 116
　respectful, 63

youth literature
　curriculum integration, 21
　provision of, 18
　rationale, 20, 49, 53, 65, 82
　selection of, 28, 30, 39, 41, 59, 80, 102, 146, 165

GPSR Compliance

The European Union's (EU) General Product Safety Regulation (GPSR) is a set of rules that requires consumer products to be safe and our obligations to ensure this.

If you have any concerns about our products, you can contact us on

ProductSafety@springernature.com

In case Publisher is established outside the EU, the EU authorized representative is:

Springer Nature Customer Service Center GmbH
Europaplatz 3
69115 Heidelberg, Germany

www.ingramcontent.com/pod-product-compliance
Lightning Source LLC
LaVergne TN
LVHW011816060526
838200LV00053B/3811